If this is mid-life...

where's the crisis?

If this is mid-life...

where's the crisis?

Sam Cook

Illustrations by Joy Morgan Dey

Pfeifer-Hamilton
Duluth, Minnesota

Pfeifer-Hamilton
210 West Michigan
Duluth MN 55802-1908
218-727-0500

If This Is Mid-Life, Where's the Crisis?

Grateful acknowledgement is made to the *Duluth News-Tribune* for permission to reprint these stories and columns, which originally appeared in that newspaper.

Printed in the United States of America

10 9 8 7 6 5 4 3 2 1

Editorial Director: Susan Gustafson
Manuscript Editor: Tony Dierckins
Art Director/Illustrator: Joy Morgan Dey

Cover photo by Jeff Frey
Author photo by Jack Rendulich

Library of Congress Cataloging-in-Publication Data

Cook, Sam.
    If this is mid-life, where's the crisis? / Sam Cook.
        p.   cm.
    ISBN 0-938586-90-4 (pbk.) : $12.95
    1. Family life—Humor. 2. Middle age—Humor. I. Title.
PN6231.F3C66   1993
814'.54—dc20   93-23267

For Sam and Libby

Acknowledgments

I am grateful for the help and support of many people in making this book possible.

This collection could not have happened if these stories had not first been published in the *Duluth News-Tribune*. It's a privilege to be able to write a column and share my views with our readers each week, and I thank the *News-Tribune* for allowing me to do it. Specifically, I am in debt to Bob Jodon, a former editor of the newspaper, whose idea it was for me to begin writing a weekly column of general interest. I thank Bob Ashenmacher and Linda Hanson, who edited these columns on a weekly basis at the newspaper.

Thanks to everyone at Pfeifer-Hamilton Publishers who had a hand in the production of this book, especially to Don and Nancy Tubesing for their continued belief in me, and to Susan Gustafson, who shepherded this book along its way to completion.

I appreciate all of those who, by word or deed, inspired these columns.

I thank Phyllis and Emily and Grant, who have permitted me to make something of a public spectacle of our family. They've held up well under the exposure. They're also wonderful people with whom to share a lifetime.

Finally, I thank my parents, Sam and Libby, whom I come to appreciate more and more the longer I'm a father myself.

—Sam Cook

Contents

Gerbils and other realities of the forties

Life as we know it

Youth soccer
and other parental rites of passage

Life is sweet

Introduction

Most Wednesday mornings, I get a little edgy. That's because every Wednesday at noon, my Friday column is due.

Some weeks, I have it finished sooner than that. But more often than not, I'm still fidgeting and rewriting and pushing words around right up until noon.

I've been enduring Wednesday mornings this way for about five years now. That's how long there's been the Friday column.

I'm sure some readers of the *Duluth News-Tribune,* where these essays first appeared, were a little surprised by my ramblings on Friday about kids and love and life. Before that, I had written mainly about fishing and hunting and other outdoor pursuits.

Fortunately, the opportunity to do the Friday column came at a good time in my life. I was on the verge of turning forty, which, as any mid-life male can tell you, offers plenty to think about. My wife and I had a four-year-old daughter and a son somewhere on the drawing board.

Phyllis and I had grown up in Kansas and quit good jobs in the mid-1970s to move north and work for a canoe outfitter in Ely, Minnesota. That was supposed to be a year-long fling in an otherwise normal life, but as often happens with major risk-taking ventures, they lead you in ways you could never have predicted.

We stayed, more or less, and now have been Minnesotans for more than a third of our lives.

I have written, most Fridays, simply about what has been on my mind. About being a dad. About being a husband. About the kind of world we live in. About television and the drawer with the leftover containers and how much money is enough money.

When I write about these things, I feel as if I am thinking out loud. They are the same kinds of things I would tell a friend at lunch. In the beginning, I felt as if these thoughts and concerns and ponderings were mine alone.

What I've come to find, through comments I get on the street and letters that readers send, is that a lot of us are thinking and wondering and laughing at the same things. We may be different in a lot of ways, but we're more the same than we'd all like to admit.

I thought I was probably the only guy who put on a good tape and danced with his three-year-old son. Nope.

I figured maybe it was just my spouse who was picky about how I did the laundry. Nope.

I didn't know so many other couples found it as difficult as we do to set aside time for each other. But they do.

Some readers, I know, have been surprised at the way I lay out the lives of my wife and children for all to scrutinize. I'm sure Phyllis, with whom I've spent twenty-one wonderful years, has been uncomfortable with this exposure at times. I do not, I assure you, publish anything I fear would be too uncomfortable for her without letting her read it first. She has the power of veto, but she has never used it.

I am perhaps more concerned about making unwilling public figures of my children. It is easier to write about them when they are too young to read, and before they have a sense of what Dad does for a living. Once they catch on to the game,

I'm inclined to leave them out of the picture. I only hope that when they discover some of these pieces in a box—or a book—when they're grown up, they'll feel I was fair to them.

Finally, I would offer this. It is a kick to be here in the middle of life, looking both ways. It is a bit like standing at the crest of a hill, looking down one way at where you came from and another at where you're going.

I'm a lucky guy. I'm having a good ride. Life is good, mostly.

S. C.

Duluth, Minnesota

Life's OK, mostly

Moving to the music

We are dancing in the living room. Just the two of us.

I'm the one in the blue jeans and T-shirt, getting ready for work. I've already had my Shredded Wheat and toast.

He's the little guy in my arms, almost three, still in his gold pajamas. They're the kind with the feet in them, and they're tattered from high mileage.

I had put the tape on because I wanted to hear one song from it. Nothing you'd recognize, probably, but I had played it the night before and couldn't get it out of my head. "Silver Thunderbird," by Marc Cohn. A tribute to a car is all it is, sung with feeling. It seems to say something about a simpler time, but I'm not seeking deeper meaning at the moment.

I'm dancing.

The little guy has his arms wrapped around my neck and his legs wrapped around my waist. He's soft and wiry at the same time, and he still smells like last night's sleep.

We have the volume cranked up good so we can feel the music.

We dance and Cohn sings.

"Don't gimme no Buick,
Son, you must take my word.
If there's a God in heaven,
He's got a silver Thunderbird."

We have a small audience. Mom is brushing the eight-year-old's hair in the next room. I can't tell if they're laughing at us or at something else. The music is too loud to hear their words. But if they're getting a chuckle at our expense, it's worth it.

We swoop all over the living room. I do things I'd never consider on a dance floor.

We spin. We dip until my boy's hair all hangs down. The cat walks through, but she doesn't seem to understand what's happening. She keeps on going.

If you know anything about almost-three-year-olds, you know they aren't likely to stay with any one thing for long. It wouldn't surprise me if he would suddenly slide from my arms and hop away to go play with his gas station.

But he doesn't.

He clings to me like a little monkey and nuzzles his face against my neck. It is one of those things that happens between a parent and a child that you can never predict, that get inside of you and bring you fully into the moment. You know, after you've been at the Dad game for a while, how rare moments such as these are, and you will do almost anything to prolong one of them.

Cohn cranks into his chorus, and the two of us whirl around the room.

"You can keep your Eldorados,
And the foreign car's absurd.
Me, I wanna go down
In a silver Thunderbird."

The music carries us away. For me, there is no more morning paper, no Shredded Wheat and bananas, no more eight-year-old's lunch to make. It's just the two of us, hugging and dancing and lost in time.

There are some things about being a parent you can see coming. Sleepless nights. Getting to know your pharmacist on a first-name basis. Putting Band-Aids on tiny hurts.

But there are moments like this one that no one could have prepared me for.

They happen when you least expect them, when you have something else in mind, or nothing in mind at all.

Suddenly you are aware of something much stronger than you ever thought it was, something palpable between you and that little mammal you helped bring into the world, and what he means to you and what you must mean to him.

It's a flash of insight so strong it almost knocks you over, but you keep on dancing so the spell won't be broken.

Which is what we did the other morning, when Marc Cohn was singing about a car.

When "Silver Thunderbird" was over, and the music stopped between cuts on the tape, the little person on my chest leaned back and looked up at me.

He said, "Another song's coming on, Dad."

We danced to it, too.

The Big 4-0

It happened quite simply. Overnight, to be precise.

He went to bed thirty-nine. He woke up forty.

He will tell you it is no big deal, being forty. Another year, that's all.

But if it's no big deal, why has he been thinking about it so much lately? And why do those who know he's forty make the cute little remarks they make?

It *is* something of a big deal, being forty. It's a passage. You get only about seven good decades in life, and there's no way around it. He's just put another one of them behind him.

A friend told him the other day, "Forty is the old age of youth and the youth of old age." Which sounds a lot like, "Business is slow in the morning, but it slacks off in the afternoon."

He remembers what he did shortly after waking up forty. He swung his legs out of bed. He looked at them. They were the kind of legs that, if you were a kid, and those were your dad's legs, you'd wonder how your mom could have fallen in love with him.

But they still work, he thought. So do his spindly arms. And his back has never gone out on him. He is no work of art, he figures, but he can still get from one end of the trail to the next.

Not that there aren't some ominous signs on the horizon. His high-frequency hearing has lost something. He can't always hear the high notes of a white-throated sparrow's call now, and he misses that.

His hair is beginning to look a little like an old black Lab's muzzle. Distinguished, he calls the look. "It's gray," his wife reminds him.

And sometimes, after those pipe-cleaner legs have pushed a little farther than they should, his knees telegraph a message to his brain: "Too far. Stop. You're not twenty anymore. Stop. You're also not thirty anymore. Stop."

So, he stops for a day or two, until the knees become friends with his brain again.

But for the most part, being forty has nothing to do with how much he can pack over a portage or what his time is in a ten-kilometer run. It has to do with being rich. And he knows he's a richer man at forty than he was at twenty, or even thirty.

It is great to be young and feel immortal. It is better, he believes, to be forty and understand the meaning of vulnerability.

That is what has happened in twenty years, as much as anything, he guesses. He has come to know that life—that living—isn't something you take for granted. He has seen life snatched away too often to feel that way anymore.

He sometimes thinks, on long runs with sore knees, about a friend who had a brain tumor. Gone at twenty-six. He thinks about an explorer who died on a mountain in Alaska. Gone at forty. He thinks about those he knows only through the printed word, who were gone before he had a chance to thank them.

And then he thinks of his own good fortune. Inevitably, it is not the accomplishments that come to mind, but simple moments, often quiet, full of significance. That last morning on the Gods River, paddling down to Hudson Bay. A midnight on Ellesmere Island, bathed in arctic light, listening to white wolves howl. Or stepping out of the snow house in the January night, gazing at a hard, white world and the star-speckled heavens—for about thirty seconds.

It is the accumulation of these fine moments, set against the backdrop of a world that is often crazy and sometimes unfair, that makes life so sweet. He is a lucky man, this fellow with the humorous legs. He knows that.

He didn't realize it at twenty. He was beginning to get the picture at thirty.

At forty, he's sure of it. He's having a good ride. He doesn't want to get off yet.

Seeing both ways

We are skiing down a frozen river, my friend and I. It is a snappy Sunday morning in January, and we have stolen away for a couple of hours to do one of the things we love.

Snow covers the river's ice. We have followed deer tracks for a while, and the deer had followed someone on snowshoes. Snowy riverbeds tell stories.

But that was earlier, when we were moving upstream. Now we are careening back down, whooping and yahooing like a couple of boys on a sledding hill. We are infected with the spirit of this river, which, like all North Shore streams, is in a hurry to make its final plunge to Lake Superior.

It occurs to me, the next time we pause to lean on our poles, that we are here in the middle of this river in the middle of winter in the middle of our lives.

This last fact is the one that pulls me up short.

I can't help thinking about my dad when he was in his early forties. I cannot imagine him doing something like this—cavorting, playing, being a little boy in the middle of life. And yet, I'm sure he did the same thing.

It must have happened on those quail hunts with Doc

Stone, his best friend. Or in a golf game with his regular foursome—the chiding, the jokes, the satisfaction of smacking a tiny ball 250 yards down the middle of the fairway.

Sure.

He must have felt the same way then that I felt dropping over that last set of frozen waterfalls, riding my skis, feeling the canyon air slipping past my face, coasting to a stop and turning to watch my buddy make the drop.

Part of it is physical—the skiing for me, the long drive dead-center down the fairway for Dad. Part of it is friendship— someone with whom to share the sweet shots and the exhilaration of a fast run. And part of it is simply being allowed to be a kid again, free of responsibilities for two hours on a river or three on a golf course.

I remember few times seeing my dad being a kid, and maybe that should come as no surprise: If I was there, he was being a dad first.

But I remember one time when I was about a first-grader. He had been passing me the football in our front yard, and when we were through, he kicked that football the way a grown-up would—just for the pure fun of kicking it.

Man, did that football go. Higher than the house. Twice as high as the house? Higher than I'd ever seen any foot-propelled object fly. I was in awe. And I'm sure my dad had done it just for fun, to see how high he could kick a football.

I find I like this middle part of life. It's like being on a knoll and being able to see both ways—back to those days as a kid and ahead to where my parents are now, gray and seasoned by the years.

I feel a closeness to my parents that I haven't felt for a long time. They seemed so old—so adult—when I was a kid. Now I realize they were just grown-up kids themselves. They happened to have three or four of us running around with noses that needed wiping and diapers that needed changing and footballs that needed pumping up.

I suppose to my child I am almost 100 percent adult, always cautioning about looking both ways at streets and requiring she at least try one bite of lasagna and urging her to be careful climbing on the banister.

Boring.

If she could only see me now on the river. We are coming to the best set of drops, little falls three or four feet high. My friend and I attack them with a series of yips and hollers, flying off the lips of the falls, occasionally sprawling on our rear ends, but mostly flying after one another down the river full of abandon.

I smile.

Someday, in the middle of her life, my child will be paddling a set of rapids or scaling some chunk of rock—or golfing. And it will dawn on her that maybe, when her dad was in the heart of his life, it didn't get much better than a Sunday in January, on a river with a friend.

Tucked in

She is down now. If not sleeping, she is at least tucked in and horizontal, snuggled up with all of her stuffed critters— Snoopy, Mickey, Gray Bear, and the gang.

I have sung her "Baa, Baa, Black Sheep" and "Twinkle, Twinkle." The night light in her room is on. So is the one in the bathroom.

All is well.

It is 8:00 P.M. I plod downstairs. My wife is sitting in the chair in the living room. It is a familiar spot for her. Two college textbooks are stacked on the arm of the chair. Another is open in her lap. The type on the pages is dense. It looks boring, even from a distance.

My wife, the student. She is on a collision course with a master's degree. The intersection will occur sometime in the next year or so, give or take the arrival of a baby.

Meanwhile, she sits in the chair with her head hung over the book. A yellow felt-tip marker reaches out, highlights a line or two of the dense type, and returns to its ready position.

We don't speak to each other at these times, the student and

I. She needs to study. I have plenty to do—some laundry, slides to edit, a loose screw to tighten in the front doorknob.

We have become good at living this way, the student and I. We are like roommates. I have my tasks. She has hers. We are efficient. We get our child to bed on time, mostly. We wear clean clothes, mostly. The student gets A's, mostly.

It has been this way for as long as we can remember, or about two years now. That's how long the student has been going to school.

Funny, this isn't the way we envisioned marriage twenty years ago when we were young and in love. Oh, to be married. After several years of dating, we would finally be together all the time. Morning. Evening. Weekends.

Paradise.

Isn't that the way you had it figured? You and your sweetheart, living together, sitting in front of the fireplace with the dog at your feet, maybe a book in your lap, planning next summer's big trip.

Then someone rewrote the script.

Let's see. It goes something like this.

Breakfast. Sack lunches. ("I only want five grapes, Dad.") Child dressed. ("I *hate* those socks, Mom.") Kid off to kindergarten. Dad to work. Student back to her book. Kid home from kindergarten. Student takes kid to day care: Snowsuit, boots, daypack. Dad picks up kid at day care: Snowsuit, boots, daypack.

Home. Kindergartner needs to set the table. ("I can't. My legs hurt.") Prepare tuna-noodle casserole. Eat tuna-noodle casserole. Clear table. Do dishes. Help kindergartner find picture of something that begins with the letter "R" for homework assignment. Kindergarten? Homework? Student gives kindergartner bath. ("Do we *have* to wash my hair?") Student reads books to child.

Dad sings. Baa, baa, black sheep. Twinkle, twinkle. Lights out. Isn't this where we came in?

We are not alone in this game, the student and I. You can see it in the eyes of people you meet on the street, or catch snippets of evidence in conversations at the office.

Most of us are two-wage-earner families. Sometimes we don't work the same shifts. Some of us are single parents. We shuttle kids to hockey practice, volunteer to make ice at 2:00 A.M., throw birthday parties, try to get the muffler fixed, help someone with his algebra, and still try to have five meals a week that don't come from a pizza place.

It's crazy.

The other night, the student and I had a date. We didn't go anywhere. The student walked away from a term paper on the word processor. I quit folding laundry. It was 10:00 P.M. We met in the living room.

"Hi."

"Hi."

For ten minutes, we had a regular conversation. We read aloud from a book we both liked. Then we talked a little more.

That was about it.

Both of us remarked later what a good time it had been.

How much is enough?

I dropped by to see a dogsledding friend of mine the other day.

He lives in the woods, not far from a river, in a two-room cabin heated only by a woodstove.

When I got there, my friend was outside. He was using an axe to chop big chunks of frozen fish parts into smaller chunks of frozen fish parts. When he had enough of the smaller chunks, he tossed them into some five-gallon pickle pails and hauled them inside.

He set them by the woodstove, where they began to thaw. Once malleable, the fish parts would be mixed with a slurry dog food that waited in a sawed-off barrel across the room.

On the other side of the woodstove, in a large metal pan, a beaver lay on his back. He was dead and furless, his exposed flesh a Swiss cheese white. His orange and curled teeth pointed toward the ceiling. His webbed feet and his flat tail hung outside the pan.

The beaver, too, was on his way to a state of thaw and to becoming the highlight of some Alaskan husky's next meal.

I call my friend a dogsledder. He is not only a dogsledder.

He is, by summer, a carpenter. But this time of year his tool belt lies in a corner of the cabin, retired. Come winter, my friend is a full-time dogsledder.

He lives simply in this cabin, with his thirty or forty sled dogs outside in their own houses. He would like to have more money, my friend says. He has thought about giving tourists rides in a remodeled bus behind his dog team as he trains them in the fall. For money.

He chuckles when he says that, but I am not sure he is joking. A man has a lot of time on the back of a dogsled to think about the cost of dog food.

My friend does not complain about his financial condition. He is living the way he wants to live. He makes some sacrifices. He is rewarded in country sunrises and in woodsmoke rising straight from his chimney on a twenty-below-zero morning and in the kind of understanding that comes between men and dogs working together.

Not long after that visit, I received a call late one night from a close friend in the lower Midwest. A corporate vice-president. He had been in the Philippines on business during the recent coup attempt. He heard the firefighting in the streets. He saw a couple of planes blow up.

He was lucky to have flown out that day, he said. He was glad to be home.

He didn't say it, but I detected he was glad to be alive.

Conversation poured out of him, and feelings. We had the best talk we have ever had. We talked about kids and old jobs and current jobs and money and happiness.

"This will blow you away," he said. "I make $90,000 a year."

I knew he was doing well. I didn't know he was doing quite that well.

"And you know what?" he said. "It isn't enough."

That blew me away.

I could tell by the tone of his voice he wasn't saying this to impress me. If anything, he sounded a bit wistful about it.

What he was getting at was that money is a relative thing. You make ninety grand a year, you find a way to spend it. Home. Cars. Kids. VISA. Duck camps. Season tickets.

It comes. It goes.

Ninety grand. Fifty grand. Fifteen grand. You make it. You spend it.

"My house payment is twelve hundred dollars a month," he said.

I thought of my friend the dogsledder. I wondered how much dog food that would buy. Or how many beaver carcasses.

The dogsledder and the vice-president. One in his cabin by the river. One in his sprawling suburban home. One with thirty or forty dogs. One with a couple of kids.

One of them wondering how to buy more dog food. One of them wondering how he can afford to join a country club.

A dogsledder sipping tea by a thawing beaver. A jet-setting vice-president delivered from chaos in the Philippines.

Both of them getting by, trying to figure out what matters. Life.

It's the craziest thing.

Working it out

Taking sides

A recent night. Eleven-thirty P.M. Second-floor bedroom.

The two of us had turned in for the night. One of us was tired and pregnant. The other was merely tired.

I'm not sure how long the light had been out. Two minutes would be a generous estimate. Then, from the darkness, came the sound of a voice I recognized as that of Tired and Pregnant.

"You're on my side," she said.

"No, I'm not," I answered.

"You are, too," she said.

We had been through this before. Roughly a billion times. I knew what was coming next.

"One, two, three and a half," she said.

She was counting the posts on our brass headboard, which divide the headboard into seven sections. Each of us is allotted three-and-a-half sections worth of mattress width.

I knew what was coming after the count, too. It came right on schedule—my honey's hand, tracing the imaginary line from three and a half sections of the headboard toward the foot of the bed.

Here came the hand now, past my ear, just missing my shoulder, and then —to my way of thinking—on a diagonal toward the closet on my side of the room. It was clearly a skewed interpretation of half a bed, but it was consistent with previous demarcations. My sweetie actually believes I regularly usurp part of her half of the bed.

(A case could be made here for someone being pregnant and thus needing more than her half of the bed. But it won't be.)

All of which helps explain why, last Sunday afternoon, the two of us were lying on a bed right out in broad daylight at an otherwise respectable home furnishings establishment in Duluth.

We had decided we had outgrown our double bed. What we needed was a larger sleeping arena.

We bounced from one queen-size bed to another, testing your six-coil springs, your five-coil springs, your steel box-spring frames, your wooden box-spring frames, your ultra-pillowed finish, and your other bedding attributes.

The sales lady was nice. She explained our options and left us alone for a while. She must have known it would be awkward to watch a couple take a few mattresses for a test-sleep.

After the sales lady rejoined us, we explained to her that we were looking for this new bedding to save our marriage—or at the very least lengthen the time we spent in bed actually sleeping.

Finally, after much bed-hopping, we decided on a mid-range, queen-size, non-pillowed, sale-priced, and rebate-qualifying mattress and box springs. We'll take delivery soon.

I would like to think our purchase will change things. I would like to think our spacious new sleeping system will prevent the necessity of our buying sheets with a dotted line down the middle.

But first things first. There will be the matter of getting a new headboard, of course. We'll need something wide enough to fit the new queen. Something with, say, eight full sections instead of only seven.

That's where I keep hitting a snag. I have this recurring image in the recesses of my brain of the two of us, lying there on our new queen, in the dark, tucked in. Subtly, I feel a knee against my leg, then a hip nudging my hip.

Somewhere in the dark, the words come floating across the room: "One, two, three"—and this time they go all the way to—"four." Then comes the hand, tracing its aberrant course across my body.

I knew we should have decided to spring for the king.

Dating game

I'll be brutally honest about it.

I'm having a dating problem.

Fortunately, it is with my wife, Phyllis, which alleviates a lot of potential difficulties.

You would think the two of us would have the dating thing pretty much down because we've been at it since high-school biology class.

Lately, though, things have been tougher, for a couple of reasons. One reason is six years old. The other is nine months old.

Here's what happens. A couple of months will have gone by, and Phyllis and I will realize that the only quality time we've spent together has been on our hands and knees in the glow of a Mickey Mouse night-light as we cleaned the carpet after a sick-child episode.

OK, we say. We need to have a date.

So we pick a night, and we call a baby–sitter, and we begin looking forward to a nice evening together.

The baby–sitter comes at 6:00. At this time, both of us are generally running around in our underwear, one of us is dripping from the bathtub, and we're playing hand-off with the nine-month-old as we take turns getting dressed.

There is nothing like finally getting dressed, making one last pass of the child, only to see the familiar beige juice come launching out of the child's mouth to land on your navy blue slacks.

OK, so let's say optimistically, we leave the house by 7:00. We get in the car, look at each other and say, "Where do you want to go?"

"I don't care," we answer ourselves. "Where do *you* want to go?"

The car usually decides. We try to make it someplace special, like Wendy's.

Wherever it is, the scenario is the same. We get there, and we're both so tired, we sort of stare at each other. All those romantic scenes we've seen in the car commercials, the perfume commercials, and the beer ads never happen to us. If we were in one of those commercials, we'd be the ones asleep in the back seat or around the beach campfire.

Of course, we never think it's going to be that way. We have, in some sort of dream state, told our baby–sitter we'd be home at 11:30 P.M., maybe midnight. Now it's 8:30, we've finished our cheeseburgers, and we have no place to go.

"We can't just go home," Phyllis says. "We have a baby–sitter!"

What we need is some place that offers commercial napping. We could go there, share a bed, pay someone about $3.50, and nap—uninterrupted by sick children—for a couple of hours, get up, and go home. But there are no napatoriums.

We could walk along the lake, but the temperature is fourteen degrees and the wind is out of the northwest at thirty gusting to a million.

We do the next best thing. We drive to Hawk Ridge, a beautiful overlook along Skyline Parkway. We look at the city. It's pretty. Three minutes pass. Maybe five. The city is still pretty.

"Well, might as well go home," I say.

So we walk in at 9:30, apologizing to our baby–sitter, who has earned $6 instead of the $10 she expected.

Something's wrong here. When I was my baby–sitter's age, I constantly stayed out too late, came home, and apologized to my parents for not being home sooner. Now, as a parent, I come home too soon and apologize to a teenager for getting home early.

What's going on?

Well, the other night we had another date. This time, we weren't going to set ourselves up for Date Failure. We had the baby–sitter come at 5:00. We told her we'd be home at 10:00, maybe 10:30. She came at 5:00. We left crisply at 5:55. We had a lovely dinner. We even drove to the mall just to walk and browse. Hey, we closed the mall down at 9:00 P.M. Are we partiers or what?

At 9:10, we found the car taking us home.

I'll give my wife credit. She wanted to stay out and party.

"Let's go to Perkins," I said.

"Let's go to Target," she said.

I yawned.

"Let's go to a bowling alley," she said.

Somehow, when we were eighteen and madly in love, I didn't envision us at forty-two, driving along at 9:30 P.M. in a minus-seven wind chill debating the pros and cons of going to a bowling alley.

Call me crazy.

I just didn't see it coming.

Leftover blues

My wife and I should have lived together before we got married. I can see that now.

It would have given us a chance to get to know each other better. I would have learned she wore socks to bed. I would have learned how she squeezes the toothpaste tube. And I would have learned about her policy on covered containers.

I'm talking about the little vessels you put leftovers in and stick into the refrigerator.

I don't know how it is at your house, but at ours there's a drawer full of these things. Old yogurt containers. Old ricotta cheese containers. Old margarine containers.

I'll tell you something about that drawer. It drives me nuts.

We must have between thirty and forty million covered containers in that drawer. They're stacked, nested, packed, and squished. Their lids are randomly tossed down sides and into cracks between the stacks.

These containers date back to the earliest days of our marriage, when Phyllis began collecting them. Phyllis grew up on a farm. She's thrifty and practical. She could no more throw out a covered container than she could give away one of our children.

So, you have the problem of sheer volume. But that's only the beginning.

Something happens when you close that drawer, I swear. The lids to all those containers mutate. So when dinner is over, and it's time to put the taco fixings in a ricotta cheese container, it is impossible to find a ricotta cheese lid for it.

Phyllis always knows when I'm having a Covered Container Breakdown. I'm flailing through that drawer. Lids are flying everywhere. Stacks of covered containers are toppling. Unusual words are coming from my lips. I can see her smiling even behind my back.

I say, "OK, smart woman. You try to find a lid for this thing." What really irritates me is that she always can.

Sure, the problem of the taco fixings has been solved for the moment, but the greater irritant is that by finding the matching lid, Phyllis justifies having kept all those jillions of containers.

The only one I can match up is an old blue Tupperware container and its lid, which we once put too close to a burner on the stove. Now it's permanently blistered and warped, but somehow it still fits. I go for it every time. But inevitably, when it's my morning to containerize the leftover pancake batter, Old Blue is already in the refrigerator with leftover Chicken Stars soup in it.

And I have another breakdown, and Phyllis smugly bails me out, and boy, does that bug me.

I suppose I could solve this problem. I could violate the unspoken tenets of our marriage and go buy the kind of containers you see at the store, with the clear bottoms so you can actually see what's in them once they're in the refrigerator. But Covered Containers has always been a domain that's sort of out of my realm. I don't feel it's my territory to be making policy in.

Hey, I'm a guy. If guys ran the world, there would be no leftovers. Oh, we might roll up a piece of meatloaf in some aluminum foil once in a while, but that would be it. The rest of it, we'd just eat until it was gone, or we'd put our plates on the floor and let the dogs finish the rest.

But no.

I wallow on in my covered container misery. My only solace in this World Without Lids is when Phyllis is gone for a couple of days. I'll open the covered container drawer. I'll look at those teetering stacks of containers. I'll smile.

And then I'll start pitching them. Pitch, pitch, pitch. Deep into the recycling sack. Containers. Lids. Lids. Containers. Do they match? Hey, what does it matter?

I never toss all of them; I always leave enough to make it look good. When I'm through, I feel a glow of real satisfaction. And a touch of guilt. Don't tell Phyllis.

High and dry

It has been a good twenty years.

OK. There are still a few things we need to work out. Like whether the toilet paper should come off the top of the roll or the bottom of the roll. But other than that, Phyllis and I have had mostly good times in the twenty years we've been married.

We passed that matrimonial milestone this week, and I couldn't help but do some serious reflecting. I thought about all those carefree early years, about the trials of major moves, about the tough times that drew us closer together.

And towels.

Mostly, I thought about the towels because ours are worn out. We got them twenty years ago as wedding gifts.

Isn't that how everyone gets towels? You send out three hundred or four hundred wedding invitations, just to close personal friends and anyone else in your parents' address book, and you get a lot of towels. Big, thick, fluffy towels in colors of the day.

For ten or fifteen years, things roll along nicely. You take showers. You dry off. Everything is fine.

Then, somewhere between fifteen and seventeen years, your towels start vaporizing. Long shreds of them dangle from the sides. The ends are frayed and spare. And you notice, when you dry your face, that you can see the bathroom light through the fabric of the towel.

Phyllis and I have a serious problem: Our marriage has outlived our towels.

Frankly, we're thinking of splitting up for a couple of years. Oh, we still love each other. After a couple of years apart, we'll get remarried—probably to each other—and we'll invite all our friends and get plenty of new towels. That ought to carry us into the 2010s or so.

That will take care of the towel dilemma. But if we think towels are the biggest problem in our twenty years of marriage, we are denying some far deeper issues.

Like those fondue pots.

If you were born after the Beatles broke up, you might not know this, but everyone who got married in 1971 got about four fondue pots.

Oh, you don't know what a fondue pot is? A fondue pot— used at elaborate fondue dinners—is basically a twentieth-century version of a cannibal meal. You put a bunch of oil in a pot, heat it up, stab some hunks of meat with spearlike utensils, dip the meat in the boiling oil, then put the meat in your mouth.

We haven't eaten a fondue meal since the late 1970s, but we still own two fondue pots and all the stabbers that go with them.

And, of course, in 1971 no newlyweds set forth into the world without TV trays.

Oh, you don't know what TV trays are? I know this will sound as if we were married when pterodactyls flew over earth, but they had these trays back then with folding legs attached to them. So when you wanted to watch "Bonanza," you set the trays up in the living room and ate your dinner in front of the TV on these little tiny tables with legs like those of a newborn colt.

Nobody watches TV while eating on TV trays anymore, but we still have our spindly little trays stuck away in some closet.

So here Phyllis and I are, trying to live a meaningful and contemporary life in the 1990s with TV trays and fondue pots and see-through towels.

It's tough.

Life will be so much better when we get married again. This time we'll do it right. We'll have a bridal registry to end bridal registries.

A Kevlar canoe.

His and hers mountain bikes.

A pair of sea kayaks.

Car roof racks.

Gaiters.

Telemark cross-country skis.

And just to be traditional about it, we'll throw in a pattern for plastic camping plates.

Oh, and towels. We'll need towels.

Short-term memory loss

Call it short-term memory loss. Happens to me all the time.

I get a phone call. It's my family, calling from Missouri. I talk to them ten, maybe fifteen minutes. My wife talks for a few minutes. We hang up.

Then it happens.

Phyllis starts asking me what they said to me. I give her all of the details I can remember, which from a fifteen-minute phone call, amount to about three.

OK, two.

"Mom and Dad are fine. My brother is leaving on a trip to Thailand for work," I report.

That's it. The rest is pretty much a blur. Don't get me wrong. I like my family. I listen. But I am apparently missing the part of my brain that allows me to reconstruct phone calls for the other person in the room with me.

Phyllis will not accept this. She can't believe I have such poor recall.

She figures with some prodding she can get more out of me.

"Well, when you said, 'Oh, really? He did?' what were they talking about?"

Hey, I tell her, I don't know. That was five minutes ago.

I can remember most of the New York Yankees' starting line-up in 1956, but I'll be darned if I can regurgitate the contents of a phone call while the receiver's still warm.

I would like to say the same is true of Phyllis, but no. She can spit out details of a phone conversation as if she were a tape recorder that someone rewound and played back.

My problem is more than a phone-call phenomenon.

If I see an acquaintance on the street whose wife has had a baby, it's a long shot whether I'll be able to remember to tell my wife when I get home. And if I do tell her, she'll invariably ask for some extraneous detail like the sex of the baby.

"Let's see," I say, stalling for time. "Hmmm. I think it might have been a boy. Boy? No, wait. Maybe he said girl. Boy or girl. Yep. It was a boy or a girl."

"You can't remember?" she says.

"Well, no."

"How big was it? Did it have hair? Who did it look like?" she asks.

She's whipping a dead horse now. She knows she doesn't have a prayer of getting an answer. She wants to watch me squirm.

I could tell her that the brook trout I caught on a lake not far from the Gunflint Trail in March 1984 weighed two and three-quarters pounds, and that I caught it on an orange teardrop jig tipped with the tail section of a dead minnow in about fifteen feet of water. I could tell her that it was a male, and that it had an iridescence that was part northern lights, part rainbow.

But someone else's baby?

Don't all babies weigh about the same? Roughly between six and nineteen pounds? Some come with hair. Some don't. Either way, it evens out. They all have hair by the time they get to kindergarten.

What does the baby look like? I'll tell you what it looks like. All babies—I include my own—look like one of two things: E.T., the extra-terrestrial, or the oldest uncle you have in your family.

"That's what the baby looked like, honey," I say. "Trust me."

Fifty-six. That was one heck of a year for the Yankees.

Whitey Ford. Don Larsen. Mickey Mantle. Hank Bauer. Billy Martin. Yogi Berra. Elston Howard. Gil McDougald. Bob Cerv. And at first base? Moose Skowron.

Larsen pitching that perfect game in the World Series. Yogi, his catcher, leaping into his arms. I was in second grade. I had an Alvin Dark baseball glove.

Funny. Seems like it was only yesterday.

Whiter whites

We met a woman we know on the street the other night. She was telling us about a bet she had made with her husband and what was at stake.

What was at stake was two weeks of laundry duty.

"And he has to do it my way," she said, fire in her eyes. "He can't ruin anything."

Hmmm. That sounded familiar.

I do a lot of the laundry in our family. I've got some experience in this field. I know your Warm Wash, Cold Rinse. I know your Tide Ultra. I know your Unscented Bounce.

And, Phyllis is quick to point out, I know how to ruin clothes.

I'd like to defend myself—and maybe our friend's husband—here.

First of all, what exactly is "ruined"? Phyllis had a pair of beige pants I remember from a while back. I couldn't decide what load to put them in, but they seemed thick, so I put them in with the towels.

They came out a really pretty shade of apricot. Phyllis didn't like the apricot. She preferred the beige.

I have some jockey shorts that used to be white. They're sort of pink now. I say, what is the big problem with that? I just make it a point not to wear them the night I play volleyball with the guys.

The point is, I'm willing to live with some altered clothing in return for some expedience in getting the laundry finished.

When I do the laundry, sorting is quick. You've got your Things That Should Be White, your Colors, and your Polypropylene Long Underwear.

That's basically it. Any other real slinky stuff—like your Wife's Underwear—can go in with the polypropylene load. All that stuff feels the same.

OK. That's the sorting. Now for the washing. You set the knob to Warm-Cold, you toss in some soap (never quite as much as the Tide box says, because I figure they're just trying to get you to use more of their product) and you close the lid.

You do your slinky stuff first, because it dries fastest. I hate having the dryer tied up for an hour or so trying to suck the moisture out of the towels when I've got the slinky stuff waiting in line.

When a load is dry, you take it up and put it on the living room floor so you can fold it while you watch the NCAA basketball tournament.

That's the way I do it.

I've seen Phyllis sorting out clothes for the wash. She has all these little piles. Colored clothes. Plain clothes. White things. Perma-pressed things. Towels and colored non-perma-pressed things. Items that need presoaking.

That's just the sorting. Then she gets downstairs and starts squirting stuff on the spots and laying the clothes aside. And presoaking. She gets the clothes in the washer and adds some special powder to them, fills the washer with water and lets them sit there for a couple hours.

I say, are we washing these clothes or giving them a bath?

I have a policy on drying clothes. Except for the Polypropylene Long Underwear, I dry everything in the dryer. Put it in. Crank it up. This, too, causes problems occasionally, in that some of Phyllis's clothes come out looking as if they fit our seven-year-old. I'm trying to improve in this area.

I really don't mind doing the laundry—my way. You can do it at home, and get some other things done at the same time. Like watching the NCAA basketball tournament.

The only thing that bugs me about the laundry is folding my wife's underwear. The people who make women's underwear must have a code that stipulates you have to make the stuff so it is impossible to tell when it's right-side out.

I'm trying to see if Christian Laettner is going to make the front end of a one-and-one free throw, and meanwhile I'm flipping this pair of shorts one way and the other, trying to see which way the flower on the front looks right. It's a poser.

And did you ever try to pile up a bunch of folded women's underwear? They slide around like Criscoed salamanders.

But I'll say this. They rarely change color. And they're hard to shrink. I respect that in underwear.

Snakes in the basement

Remember just when you thought Indiana Jones and his beautiful sidekick were out of trouble, and then they opened that trap door in the floor and saw the pit full of asps?

Remember how the asps were about two feet deep and wall-to-wall, writhing and hissing and slithering around on each other?

Welcome to our basement.

And so, Phyllis and I stood there, looking down last Saturday, wondering where to start.

We didn't actually have snakes down there, understand. Not that we knew of, anyway. But after you've lived in a place for five years or so, and you just keep setting things "over in that corner of the basement," there comes a time when, if you're honest with yourself, you *don't know* what's living down there.

Let's take a walk through the model basement now. On your right, under the stairs, is the cardboard box emporium. The ones we save in case we need to mail something to someone. Hey, I'll bet L.L. Bean doesn't have this many boxes under *his* basement stairs. Big boxes. Little boxes. Parts of cut-up boxes. Boxes that have been play cars, with headlights and horns drawn on them and doors cut out of their sides.

The boxes are stacked on top of our heirloom cane chairs, the ones the cane has been out of since we inherited them. The ones we'll surely get around to recaning one of these decades. I can see it now. Our retirement. We'll finally have replaced the cane and have the chairs on an actual occupied level of the house, where our friends and guests can see them. Our friends will come over and say, "Wow, these are beautiful cane chairs. What smells like mold?"

That will be the same smell you're smelling now, on the basement tour, where we see the fifty-pound sack of dog food on your left. It has been sitting there, leaning against the basement wall, since Dave, our black Irish setter, died about four years ago. It's been waiting for that new dog we will get. Mostly, though, it's been getting more and more humid, until— well, here, let's just pull it out from the—WATCH OUT! DOG FOOD AVALANCHE!

That's right. The soggy basement gremlins rotted that dog food sack, and now we have dog food in the old baby food jars, dog food in the paint roller tray, dog food in the gardening water cans and the steel wool and the canning jars.

Which is pretty much where Saturday started.

But we were committed. We waded into those asps and got after them.

I performed Greco-Roman Olympic events with some old mattresses that had an appointment with the landfill. Phyllis scooped dog food and smashed cardboard boxes and recycled baby food jars and chased Styrofoam packing peanuts around the basement.

Of course, we had a few of our traditional differences over what to save and what to keep. The Lupine Blue paint, for instance. We actually chose this color for our inside back porch, thinking it would look Swedish or something. What it looked like was the way the inside of your stomach feels when you've been on Lake Superior too long in a big sea.

Finally, I thought—we'll throw it out, haul it down to the city's Household Hazardous Waste center with the rest of our old paint. Silly me. I should have known. Phyllis wanted to save it.

Phyllis and I were born with different sets of genes on the scale of saving things or throwing them out. I tend to throw out almost anything we don't use on a daily basis. Phyllis will hold onto things we haven't used since shortly after we got married— like that ball of jute twine she used for macrame projects in the early '70s.

I couldn't get rid of that on Saturday, either.

But we made a lot of headway in that temple of doom. My high point might have been heaving those mattresses into the landfill that morning. They smelled like the basement, and the stuffing was bulging out of them in a couple of spots, and they were stained and gray and ugly. Our eight-year-old looked on as I slung them to their final resting place.

When we got back in the car to leave the landfill, she was quiet for a moment. Then she said, "I feel bad putting those mattresses out there with all that *garbage*, Dad."

I shuddered.

I should've known which set of genes would get passed on.

Give and take

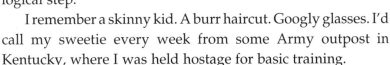

Marriage.

You wouldn't think it would be so tough, would you?

A man. A woman.

They fall in love. Marriage seems the next logical step.

I remember a skinny kid. A burr haircut. Googly glasses. I'd call my sweetie every week from some Army outpost in Kentucky, where I was held hostage for basic training.

I lived for those calls. All I wanted was to be home. With her.

All I wanted was to be married. Everything would be great.

A year or so later, when I was wearing normally colored clothes again, we were married. It *was* great. It wasn't quite what I had imagined, but it was pretty close.

The illusion, of course, was that once we were married, we'd be able to spend all our time together. No more driving home late at night to sleep in our own beds. No more long weekend commutes to be with the ones we love. No more long-distance phone calls.

But reality rears its head. In most marriages, especially young ones, both partners work. You get up in the morning, a little later than you should. You race around for an hour or so, making yourself presentable for the rest of the world. You spend eight or nine hours with the rest of the world. You come home. You're tired. You're hungry. Somebody forgot to thaw out the chicken.

Welcome to the real world of marriage.

Throw in a kid or two, a few hundred stops at day care, maybe some night classes toward a master's degree, and it's easy to see why some people feel more like roommates than husbands and wives.

I was thinking about all of this because I've spent some time recently with two couples who seem to have good marriages. After each visit, I came away sort of inspired about the institution.

In the case of each couple, it wasn't an outward show of affection that told me they were in love. It was a sense of quiet appreciation of one another. It was the way they spoke to each other—when they agreed, when they disagreed.

You could tell they respected each other. There was a tolerance at work between those spouses, a willingness to give a little, to allow another his or her differences.

None of these qualities was exhibited over large issues. It was the little places where it showed. One was a short debate over the correct temperature at which to bake trout.

The longer I'm married, the more often I think it comes down to those kinds of things. I can remember being involved in discussions—OK, arguments—with my wife over equally trivial matters.

I'm not sure why it seems so important to win some of those little battles, why we dig our heels in so hard and hold out for our way. I remember hearing one of the recently released Western hostages talking about disagreements he had had with one of his fellow hostages.

One of their arguments, he said, was about airplanes at

takeoff and whether their flaps were in the up or down position. They had had quite an argument about it. The hostage being interviewed said it wasn't just that they disagreed, but that neither had been willing to admit that the other could possibly have been right.

Tolerance. A willingness to give a bit.

I would throw one other quality in there—the ability to say you're sorry. Sometimes, we are so hung up on winning and losing, we can't admit it even when we're wrong. Or tougher yet, admit we were jerks about something even when we were right.

Perhaps you detect in there a voice speaking from experience.

One last thing. I think we expect our marriages to work simply because we fell in love, once, a long time ago. I've often thought that keeping a marriage on sound footing shouldn't be so darned *hard* at times.

But it is.

And it's worth it.

Transition hairstyles and other issues

Transition hair

I once married a woman who had long, straight hair. Brunette. Not down to her waist or anything, but long. It blew in the wind and looked good wet and I fell in love with her in biology class and we got married.

The same woman walked in the other night after coming home from the beauty shop. Her hair was chopped at the neck. The rest of it was swirled and piled so high and so far back I thought maybe she'd been caught in a cotton-candy machine. It looked as if her hair had been designed by an extremely active group of hornets.

She spun around once in the kitchen.

"How do you like it?" she asked. "Whitney Houston."

All I can say is I'm glad she told me because "Whitney" and "Houston" probably wouldn't have been the first two words out of my mouth.

Don't get me wrong. She didn't go cold turkey from long and straight to Whitney and Houston.

There have been years of what a friend of hers likes to call "transition" hairstyles.

My wife would compliment her friend on a new haircut, and her friend would say, "Oh, thanks, but it isn't exactly what

I wanted. Jim said I had to let the sides get longer before he could shape the back. Then he's going to frost the top and perm me. This is just to get me by until it grows out a little."

My wife would nod. I think she actually understood because her hair was probably in transition at the time, too.

Jim, of course, is the hairstylist. Jim has a plan. He knows where a woman's hair is going. Jim must have extensive notebooks at work full of personalized hair plans for women. The plans must have flowcharts and spreadsheets and timetables.

This whole matter of evolving hairstyles is kind of a mystery to those of us who don't have long-range hair plans, except maybe to keep most of it.

I will admit I go to a hairstylist. Her name is Terri. According to a plaque on her shelf, she was stylist of the month for several months running at the shop where she works.

It must be frustrating for such a talented person to deal with someone like me.

"How would you like it?" Terri asks as I settle into the chair.

"Same as always," I say.

She shampoos. She snips. She trims.

Twenty minutes later, I'm done.

Oh, Terri tries to drag me into the nineties. When she finishes my ho-hum cut, she can't resist taking a funky brush and brushing all my hair back toward the top of my skull.

I suppose I look quite dashing, like one of those catalog guys, for about three minutes. That's how long it takes to get my check written and get outside. Then, with licked fingers, I go about returning my hair to the seventies.

On occasion, late in the day, I have gone straight home from Terri to my wife. I'll enter the room as Catalog Guy, strike a beach-volleyball pose from the Eddie Bauer catalog and try to make my eyes look real blue and distant.

And Phyllis will say, "Boy, you have a lot of forehead. You remind me of your cousin Randy."

I immediately go upstairs and shampoo my hair into submission.

Which brings us back to my wife, Whitney Houston. This latest hairdo is just one in a series of styling surprises she has come home with over the past few years. Most have been perms. Perm, near as I can tell, is a hairstyling word that means "fifty-five dollars."

I have learned, by watching, that you don't comb a perm. What you do, when your hair is wet, is bend over at the waist until all of that squiggly hair is hanging down. Then in one whiplash-like motion, you raise your body to its upright position and snap your head back.

There. Your perm is combed. Whitney does this all the time in our bathroom.

OK. I need to be fair here. Phyllis did not go to get her haircut seeking the Whitney Houston look. I think her stylist named it that.

Watching me circle her warily in the kitchen, Phyllis assured me her hair would—these are her words—"come down."

I really wasn't worried. I figured it was just a transition cut anyway.

Mom,
hanging ten

I should have seen it coming.

Phyllis has been talking about a skateboard all summer. At first it was just sort of a fascination as she watched the junior-high boys who went rolling by our home each evening.

"I'd like a skateboard," Phyllis would say.

She said it often. I would just nod or say something noncommittal or chuckle.

Remember, Phyllis is not an adolescent daughter. She is the woman with whom, seventeen years ago, I stood in a church and made various commitments, none of which said anything about what happens when the other party is thirty-nine years old, a mother of one, and wants to get pink high-topped tennis shoes and a skateboard.

But suddenly, we were standing in a checkout line, and Phyllis was clutching a hot pink skateboard and smiling.

"It's marked down from thirty dollars to twenty dollars," she said.

Being the sensitive male I am, I smiled back and said, "I don't think you need a skateboard."

To which Phyllis said something about me not needing the fly rod I bought this summer, either.

The check-out lady rang up the skateboard.

Phyllis decided not to make her maiden skateboard trip down the hill where the junior-high boys coast past our house. We went to a nearby parking lot, where she'd have plenty of room. We hadn't been there long when three boys walked by carrying their skateboards up the hill. Phyllis ran after them.

"Hey, guys," she said.

I looked the other way.

"Hey, guys. I just got this skateboard. Can you give me some tips?" she said.

The boys looked the other way, too.

"Hey, really," she said. "I need some help."

They were in a spot. It's tough to be cool when you're fourteen, out with the boys, and some woman who could be your mother wants to be your buddy.

One of the boys must have figured the best course of action was to go ahead and help this woman and then boogie. He walked her to the top of the hill.

"Sit down," he said.

"What?" Phyllis said.

"Sit down on your board," he said. "Now, just lean when you want to turn."

She scooted twice with her feet, hauled them on board and rolled down the street. It was something like watching a two-year-old in a sled coasting down a gentle incline. Which is to say, Phyllis wasn't going to get any bugs in her teeth at that speed.

By the time she reached the bottom of the hill, the boys were gone. But a skateboarder had been born.

Next thing I know, Phyllis has arranged with some fourteen-year-old named Matt to take a skateboarding lesson the following week.

"Get some pads," Matt had said. "Elbow pads, knee pads—and a helmet."

Phyllis agreed to pay Matt $3 for a half-hour lesson. That seemed a little steep to me, especially considering we pay our most trusted neighborhood girls only $1.50 to care for our daughter for a whole hour.

"Yeah, it might be a little high," Phyllis admitted.

Matt showed up last Tuesday night. His high-tops were black. His boom box was at idle.

Out came Phyllis. She was wearing elbow pads, knee pads, and a white hockey helmet she had borrowed. She looked—how can I say this?—silly as heck. Our three-year-old watched her walk by, no doubt wondering, *Is this the woman who sings me "Twinkle, Twinkle" when I go to bed?*

The lesson began with short runs down a grassy hill. Phyllis wasn't bad. Matt didn't give a lot of instruction. He mostly stood by, talking about the time he broke his wrist skateboarding.

Phyllis did the hill about forty times. Then she tried another grassy hill. The lesson culminated with Phyllis making a stand-up run down the street in front of our house.

It was a good run. Long, straight, and under control. The three-year-old and I sat on the sidewalk and watched. When Phyllis finished, we cheered. Phyllis came walking back up the sidewalk and joined us.

There we were—the typical American family. A child, a father—and a mother wearing knee pads, elbow pads, and a white hockey helmet.

I see no way to prevent the purchase of pink high-tops.

Seven months and counting

It is 9:00 P.M. My sweetie has taken her position.

It's a familiar position. She is lying on the couch. One leg is propped up on the arm of the couch. The other is thrown up over the back.

Maybe you have seen this position. Maybe you have lived with a woman who announces about once a week: "Every man should have to be pregnant at least once in his life."

Or her second-favorite quote: "Any woman who thinks being pregnant is the most wonderful thing that ever happened to her has never played a good game of handball."

It is something, this pregnancy thing.

I'm not complaining, understand. I know that, as a man, I've got nothing to complain about. It isn't my belly button that has turned from an insy to an outsy over the past few months. And I haven't heard lately of any guys who started gagging while brushing their teeth in the morning.

But the fact is, being a husband of a pregnant woman has its weird moments.

Take the bed, for instance. Last fall we bought this new, queen-size bed after spending eighteen years of marriage staking out our territories in a regular double bed. Now Phyllis hates to sleep in the new one.

"It's so hard," she says. "It hurts my back when I sleep in it."

And so, as a husband, I have this nightly debate about whether to sleep with my wife in our old, soft bed or to sleep alone in the new, hard bed. I thought the old bed was small before, but that was nothing compared to sharing it with someone who's sleeping for two.

Then there's the wardrobe problem. Phyllis has been lucky. Several friends have passed along to her their maternity clothes. But every week, as her body expands, she tries on some top, looks in the mirror and says, "Well, I can't wear this anymore."

Here at the seven-month mark, my honey has two outfits. One is casual—pink sweat pants and a pink sweatshirt. The sweats aren't really an outfit. They're more like a uniform. When I see my honey in my mind's eye, in position on the couch, it is always in the pink sweats.

By day, she wears the jeans that have sort of an expando-sunroof panel in them that allows her to adjust them to her state of expansion.

"Well, these jeans are on their last set of snaps," Phyllis said the other night. "I'm *not* going to get any new jeans. I'll add Velcro strips to these if I have to."

I suspect most pregnant women feel the same way. You see someone walking around eight-and-a-half months pregnant and my hunch is her clothes are held together mostly with rubber bands, string, or pieces of elastic scavenged from a sewing kit.

The guy's role at this stage of the pregnancy is merely to answer questions. They aren't difficult questions.

"Can you see the bottom of my stomach? Are there any stretch marks down there?"

"Are these pants too short?"

"Is it hot in here, or is it just me?"

It's an interesting time for us men.

Somewhere during this gestation period, the woman gets what is called a nesting instinct. She starts coming up with all kinds of ideas about what dressers need to be stripped and refinished for the baby's room, what woodwork needs to be stained, and how we ought to get some unfinished furniture and work it up for the kid's room.

Trouble is, every can of paint or stain or stripper comes with large-print instructions saying that pregnant women shouldn't be in the same hemisphere as these chemicals.

How come the woman gets the nesting instinct and the man ends up building the nest?

But I don't mean to make pregnancy seem like it's all a big hassle. There are some beautiful moments that come with it.

Like when we're both lying in bed at night, and the baby starts moving. Phyllis will say something like, "The baby's moving. Want to feel it?"

I do, of course.

And it's just a short walk down the hall to her bedroom.

I was a jerk

I was a jerk in high school.

Not for long. Just a few months.

I worked at a drugstore that still had fountain service. I was a soda jerk.

In case you're less than about twenty-five years old, I'll explain what a fountain is because it's likely you've never seen one.

Soda fountains were places

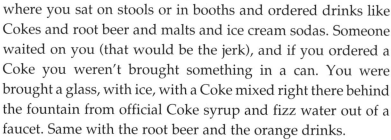

where you sat on stools or in booths and ordered drinks like Cokes and root beer and malts and ice cream sodas. Someone waited on you (that would be the jerk), and if you ordered a Coke you weren't brought something in a can. You were brought a glass, with ice, with a Coke mixed right there behind the fountain from official Coke syrup and fizz water out of a faucet. Same with the root beer and the orange drinks.

The malts were made on wonderful green machines with the name "Hamilton-Beach" on the front, and they came in large metal cans. The malt was poured from the can into a thick malt glass, and there was always leftover malt in the can. The jerks mixed the malts, too. It made a lot of noise, but it was good noise, not the kind of noise you hear at fast-food places when the french fries are done.

But fountains weren't cool just because of the drinks and the fact that someone made them for you. They were the place to be.

In our small town, high school kids hung out there, mostly after school or on Saturday mornings.

I was thinking about my days as a jerk the other night when I saw two young people apparently having a date. They were sitting at a table, watching a television screen approximately five feet wide and ten feet away, on which music was playing and a devilish-looking woman writhed seductively.

That didn't happen much at Darville's Rexall Drug Store.

When a boy and a girl had a date at Darville's, what they did was order one malt or one Coke or one root beer—and two straws. They'd sit there, sipping from opposite sides of the booth, and—I know this will sound odd—they looked right at each other.

This actually happened.

Now, I'm not saying dating was better in the Fountain Service Epoch. I'm just saying kids looked at each other instead of at something across the room and maybe even held hands under the table, which, when you're sixteen and your hormones spend most of the day doing freestyle skiing in your veins, doesn't seem like a bad deal.

We had another thing going for us then—cars without center consoles.

You'd leave the drugstore and get in your parents' 1965 Chevy Impala and the girl would sit right in the middle of the seat. There might have been two rolls of baling twine and a DeKalb Seed Corn cap in the back seat, but on a warm night with the moist air coming in the window and the smell of your sweetie's perfume blending with the scent of baling twine and maybe some brome hay dust on the front floor mats—well, life was good.

I'm not saying you can't manage to fall in love watching Madonna pretend she's a boa constrictor in a neon terrarium. I'm sure the skiers in your veins will see to it.

But somewhere along the way, you owe it to yourself to sit down with your baby someplace without an excessive amount of electricity and study the shape of each other's faces and maybe mess with each other's hair for a good twenty minutes or so.

The malt is optional, but if you get one, ask for two straws.

Nightfall in Paris

I knew it was prom season when we went out to dinner the other night.

The two young couples seated across from us were wearing roughly six hundred dollars worth of prom-related clothing, bangles, tans, and hair.

Whereas my wife and I were going to drive home, pay our baby–sitter, and try to get a decent night's sleep, these kids across from us were going to dance at least a couple of dances at the actual prom, get into some more comfortable clothing, probably hit two or three other parties, likely walk on a beach, and maybe watch the sunrise.

But that wasn't what they were doing at the moment.

At the moment, one of the guys seemed to be trying to impersonate Tom Cruise. Why else would he have been wearing sunglasses in a place already lit so dimly you could hardly read the menu?

That's to say nothing of the two young women, one of whom seemed to be concentrating mostly on remaining inside of her strapless dress.

Of all the rites and rituals of the high school years, Prom Night is surely one of the strangest and most wonderful of all.

I remember Phyllis on the night of our prom. This was about thirty or forty years ago, it seems, in a high school gymnasium that through the miracle of crepe paper and cutout stars had been converted from a place where I played B-team basketball into "Nightfall in Paris."

That transformation in itself was remarkable. There we were—right on the free-throw line where I made both of my career points in high school basketball—eating dinner in France. We probably had French fries and French dressing and everything. I don't recall.

But mostly, as a guy, I was transfixed by the transformation that had taken place in my girl. That would be Phyllis.

Here was this girl whom I knew mostly in a pair of cutoff jeans and a sleeveless blouse driving a tractor while I helped her dad bale hay. And, whoa! I showed up to pick her up on Prom Night, and here was this woman-child in some yellow lacy dress that revealed things about Phyllis I had never noticed on the tractor.

And her hair. It was piled up on her head in windrows and ringlets. It cascaded down to her bare neck in delicious curls. There was more hair there than I'd ever seen before, including a corkscrew-like twist in front of each ear.

"What are those?" I asked.

"Wispy tendrils," she said.

It was at that moment that I realized boys and girls came at Prom Night from distinctly different perspectives. I suspect the trend continues wherever night falls on Paris these days.

For us guys, it was primarily a matter of going to Hughes Clothing, getting some new socks and maybe a shirt, and throwing on the only suit we owned. Oh, and washing the car. I thought the object was to look pretty much like yourself, except spiffed up.

But I could see, by the time we got to the Free-Throw Line

in Paris, that all of the girls in our class had become someone else for Prom Night. Mostly this was done with hair, and with liberal assists from mild sunburns, sparkle mascara, and dresses that seemed to stay on despite the force of gravity.

Like the Super Bowl, the prom itself is sometimes a letdown. I know for me, it just didn't seem like Paris with Mr. Martin, the science teacher, leaning against one of the lampposts.

But Prom Night—the *night*—rarely disappoints. Sooner or later, you've changed into more conventional clothing, which feels great after being duded up. You're off with a few friends doing whatever it is kids do on Prom Night, which is mostly being hopelessly in love or something reasonably close to it.

And realizing that it's a lot harder than you thought to stay up until the sun rises.

Cold feet

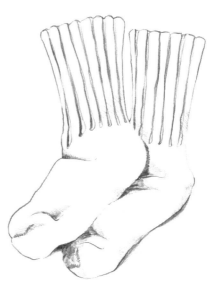

I slid into bed the other night, pulled the covers up, snuggled up to my sweetie— and detected something unusual down near the foot of the bed.

What was down there didn't feel like Phyllis's feet. They didn't feel smooth and bony. They felt vaguely furry, as if maybe a couple of muskrats had taken up residence down between the sheets.

I had felt that feeling down there before.

"Are those socks?" I asked.

"Yes," she said. "I'm freezing."

There are lots of ways to note the coming of fall—the hawk migration, the color of maple trees, salmon running in the streams.

But none of these events is official. They're influenced by the length of daylight hours, northwest winds, or rainfall. They can cover a broad spectrum of time from August through November.

I can tell you exactly when fall begins.

It begins the night Phyllis wears socks to bed for the first time, migrates over to my side of the bed, and says, "I'm freezing."

The socks will be a regular between-the-sheets feature from now until sometime in May. I don't know if Phyllis wears the same ones each night, washes them weekly or monthly, or changes colors on a nightly basis. I never see her nighttime socks. I only feel them.

I don't know if she sheds them during the night, after her feet warm up, or if she wears them until morning.

All I know is that the summer is over. And I'm going to miss it.

It wasn't that I got such a kick out of waking up in the middle of the night and realizing my bare foot was touching Phyllis's bare foot. It's just that her socks are symbolic of a lot of layering to come—long underwear, ear flaps, insulated boots, scarves, and mittens.

A person can go weeks at a time up here in the winter and not see his own bare body in the light of day.

As predictable as the Coming of the Socks is in Phyllis's life, it always takes me by surprise. It isn't the kind of thing that unfolds in stages, the way the fall colors do. One night, everything is fine. The next night—socks.

Now don't get me wrong. I don't mind the socks. I'd prefer bare feet, sure. But I've always liked muskrats, too.

It just amazes me that Phyllis can get so cold so fast. We'll be downstairs, sitting around, apparently comfortable. Then, somehow, in the time it takes to go upstairs, brush our teeth, and get into bed, she's freezing.

She's never "chilly."

She's never "cold."

She's always "freezing."

And it isn't just her feet.

Her hands are usually freezing, too. I'll be lying there, rubbing my feet against her socks, pondering the months of insulation ahead, when Phyllis's hands will come stealing over.

Somewhere beneath the covers, like a couple of rubber gloves that were filled with water and left in a freezer, they move, seeking heat. I never feel them coming. All of a sudden, they're just there, pawing at my soft underbelly.

"Warm my hands up," Phyllis says.

What follows is some rather brisk undercover evasion that never totally thwarts the Hands from Reykjavik.

Let's face it—if a good part of your body is exposed and someone with fingers like tentacles of antarctic kelp is lying inches away, you've got no defense. You're going to suffer.

I suppose it could be worse. It apparently hasn't occurred to her that she could apply the same logic to her cold-hands dilemma that she does to her cold-feet problem.

That's good. There's no way I'm sleeping with a woman wearing gloves.

And then there were four of us

Dining with Bert and Ernie

For a long time, I denied it. I thought I was still in control of my life.

I know better now.

My life has been taken over by a small person, infiltrated by the trappings of life as perceived by a five-year-old's brain.

The evidence is before me constantly.

I eat many of my meals on a Bert and Ernie placemat.

In the living room, what once served as a coffee table has now been layered with kids' blankets. From under the top blanket protrudes a bald plastic head bearing a shock of synthetic hair. The doll smiles vacantly at the ceiling. The coffee table has become a baby's changing table.

I tried to pick up a briefcase that had been lying on the living room floor for a couple of nights. It was flat across the top of an old ice-cream bucket that is now filled with crayons. When I tried to pick up the briefcase, I was scolded by the small person.

"Dad," she said scowling. "Put that back. It's part of my washing machine."

Oh. Sure.

And you know what? I put it back.

That's the crazy part. I have come to believe in these imaginary washing machines and changing tables.

I was scavenging in my closet for a pair of shoes not long ago. I found them and tried to shove my foot in one. Something was living there. It was a stuffed mouse. I removed the furry creature so I could wear the shoes—but I apologized to it.

There's nothing wrong with a grown man talking to stuffed animals in his closet, is there?

Fortunately, most of this lifestyle that has been superimposed on my own has been confined to the privacy of my home or closet. I fear that this is changing. Last weekend, we were at the grocery store and my five-year-old was transformed into a school crosswalk guard.

"You wait here," she said. "I'll walk ahead and tell you when it's safe to come."

This wasn't in the street, you understand. It was in produce. So I stood there until my crosswalk guard had her invisible flag extended. Then I safely crossed from the oranges to the broccoli, and we went on shopping.

Luckily, no other shoppers in the area were run over, either.

I wouldn't cooperate in all of these scenarios except that they seem so reasonable. Half the time we play crosswalk guard, I ask which direction the cars are coming from. The crayon container with the briefcase on top *does* resemble a washing machine. A shoe is a nice place for a mouse to live.

My small person has imposed nearly all of this make-believe life on me without malice or judgment. The only time I suspected any trickery was when she surreptitiously plastered a dinosaur sticker on the hip pocket of my jeans. I walked around for half a day before I got home and discovered the brontosaurus on my behind.

Quickly, I recapped my afternoon's travels. Bait shop. Drug store. Hardware store. Gas station.

Oh, well.

I'm hoping the dinosaur incident was an isolated thing, a token effort at intentional embarrassment.

The rest of it I can handle.

Like the other day, when I had fixed myself a sandwich and was moseying into the family room to watch a little basketball on television. I noticed immediately something was wrong. All of the lights were out and the curtains were drawn.

I turned on the TV.

"Dad," came a voice filled with frustration. "You can't watch TV."

I looked around. There was the small person in the corner, sitting on her yellow chair, wearing a dress-up dress and black pumps two sizes too large.

She had a yellow-haired doll on her lap and a bottle pointed at its immovable lips.

"I'm a day-care mom, and this is the bedroom. My babies are sleeping," she said.

Like, jeez, Dad, how could you not have noticed?

"Sorry," I said, tiptoeing out of the room.

I scooted back to the dining room table and enjoyed a quiet lunch with Bert and Ernie.

The human fireboat

It's 2:30 A.M.

I am standing in a stupor in a dimly-lit bedroom. In front of me, a tiny stream of warm liquid is spurting toward the ceiling. I am trying to suppress it with one hand. The liquid hits my hand like a stream from a garden hose aimed up at the bottom of an umbrella.

The spurting is warmer than I would have guessed. It lasts for what seems like a long time.

The source of this anointment is roughly seven pounds of human life. It is a boy human, of course. No girl is equipped to put that kind of trajectory on a liquid discharge.

We are between diapers, the boy and I. When the squirt gun has spent its ammunition, I begin the mop-up, trying to remember not to wipe the sleep from the corner of my eye with my deflector hand.

We have had worse moments, the seven pounder and I. He has, in split seconds between other diapers, hosed down the wall, my shirt, his shirt, and his face.

I had a fireboat I played with in the bathtub as a kid. It was the kind that pumped real water from a real little hose. My brother and I spent most of our formative years putting out imaginary harbor fires when we were supposed to be washing the sand out of our hair.

I had forgotten all about that fireboat until this boy came into our lives.

You can say all you want about dads and kids having quality time over a bottle of formula in the middle of the night. You can talk all you want about male bonding between fathers and sons.

Somehow, I pictured the two of us in a canoe together, tossing Shad Raps at the shoreline. Or hunkered against a well-placed log in front of a campfire.

I did not picture the fireboat at 2:30 A.M.

The trajectory problem is a mere diversion in this whole wee-hour agenda. There are more serious problems. Like, who in the heck is in charge of arranging the snaps on those baby outfits?

The rest of the world is sleeping, you've got seven pounds of raging fury wailing at you, your left hand is still dripping, and you've got to solve a logic problem posed by a set of snaps and flaps that will not match up. Tell me if I'm wrong, but it's my theory that somewhere in a generic baby-wear manual is a line that says, "No two baby outfits may possess the same pattern of snap closures."

Assuming you solve that problem, it's down the stairs, mix the formula, heat the bottle, remember to shut off the burner, and head back upstairs for the feeding.

The feeding is the only predictable part of the game. While I try to maintain consciousness, the seven pounder sucks down that formula like it's a Cherry Coke. Two ounces, and it's half-time.

Up on the knees he goes, at which time a sound something like "EERRRRAAAUUUUCH" rises from the depths of the boy, often accompanied by a white matter whose half-life is longer than bathroom tile grout.

Back down he goes for two more ounces.

Then, when you want the little human to get that half-mast look to his eyelids and slump against your chest, he turns into Mr. Wide-Eyes. All you can think of is your bed, those warm covers, and how few hours remain until you have to get up for work.

But no. The seven pounder's hairless head is bobbing around like a dashboard-mounted compass. His eyes look like two cat's-eye shooter marbles, and they have this look in them that says, "Dad, you're my man. Finally, some time alone. Let's talk. Let's have some quality time."

So, we do some male bonding, he and I.

We look into each other's eyes. We plan pebble searches and canoe trips and pheasant hunts. We vow always to talk, even when he's a teenager.

It's a beautiful moment.

I know it means a lot to him. He looks up at me, eyes gleaming, and says, "EEERRRAAAUUUCH."

Interior decorating

What baffles me is why some people pay interior decorators to redecorate their homes when you can have it done for free.

All you have to do is get a ten-month-old child.

We've had our ten-month-old for about ten months now. Early on, he wasn't much help at home decorating. That was when he was concentrating on scientific research. He spent weeks conducting sleep-deprivation experiments on his parents. Now he's beyond that and into a more creative line of work.

Picture a pudgeball of a person sitting in the middle of the living room. Picture the striped pullover shirt. Picture the blue corduroy overalls, well-worn at the knees. Picture the pudgy feet, one with a sock on, one with a sock off. Picture two blunt fangs beginning to protrude from his upper gums. Picture a pudgy chin glazed with fresh drool. Picture busy eyes, fast hands, and an iron grip.

You've got it.

Now I'll add what I perceive to be the thoughts passing through this small person's brain during a typical morning.

"What's the problem in this room? Yep. Too much visible carpeting. I thought I had it covered last night when they put me to bed. Oh, well, might as well get to work.

"Better knock over this basketful of toys. There. That's a start. Fisher-Price phone over there. Good. Gumby chew toy over there. Stuffed rabbit here.

"Oh, who put that nice miniature braided rug back on top of the trunk? There, got it. Drag it off. Let it fall. Looks good on the floor. Natural-like.

"And what about these arm covers on the overstuffed chair? Down they go. Yeah. I like it. Now, time to drag the Jr. Police Car to the middle of the room. Lot of work, but it's worth it. It's big. Big and blue and orange, and the horn honks. Better tip it over. Looks too normal with its wheels on the floor. There. Wait. Lemme gnaw on that tire for a minute. Yeah. That feels good.

"Whoops, threw another sock. Oh, well. One of the large people will come by in a minute, pin me down, and put it back on.

"Still too much carpeting showing. Needs blocks. Seven, eight, ten, twelve. Red, blue, green, yellow. They sure look good with gold carpeting.

"Now, how's the kitchen looking? Better crawl out there and check it out. Oh, no. My worst fear. Way too tidy. Drawer. Try the drawer with covered containers. Oh, look in there. Must be hundreds of them. They have to go. All of them. Let's see. Yogurt container first. Oh, look at it roll. Peanut butter container. That one rolled all the way to the dishwasher. Margarine container. Zing! Cool Whip container. Cottage cheese container. Tupperware thing. Ricotta cheese container. Zing. Zing. Zing. Zing. Now for some lids. Go, lids. Roll, lids. Lids, lids, lids. Lids everywhere.

"Shoes. What are all those shoes doing arranged neatly on that rug by the door? Here. Let me drag this boot over by the stove. Good. Now a ski boot out by the Cool Whip container. Nice. Ooh, that shoestring looks good. Time out. Gotta suck on that shoestring for a while. Man, that's good. But there's work to be done. Good thing I've got time for all of this. It's a never-ending job.

"Catalogs. I love catalogs. That nice big pile on the bottom shelf of the cart. Whing. Look at 'em slide. Catalogs and magazines. Avalanch! All right. Nice, slick paper, too. Good for chewing. I think I'll chew some *Field and Stream* today. Boy, this is slow. When am I going to get some more teeth so I can pick up the pace?

"Well, the kitchen looks good. Better pad on out to the dining room. Did someone leave the mail on the table? I think . . . I . . . can . . . just . . . about . . . reach—there, got it. Wow, what a shower of mail. I'll eat some now and save some for after my nap. Mmmm. This is good. What is it? Oh, a Homestead Tax Form. Can't be important.

"Oh, oh. Here comes Dad. Hey, big boy, where we going in such a hurry? Up the stairs. Around the corner. Oh, the bathroom. Should have figured.

"Well, while Dad's busy, I'll get this wastebasket emptied. Good stuff. Used Band-Aids. Used Kleenex. Old dental floss. This is my kind of place. Oh, come on, Dad. I was just getting started. Oh, well. I can always chew on the bathtub. Love the feel of that cool porcelain. So good on the teeth and gums.

"Hey, what's that noise? Sounds like a cross between a waterfall and a geyser. Where we going, Dad? Back downstairs? Good. I wasn't finished there yet.

"Thanks for the lift, Old Man. Sock? What sock? Don't ask me, pal. I haven't seen it since before the covered-container drawer. Oh, you found it. OK, OK, but make it fast. I see there's a Santa Claus taped to the closet door. That has to come down. Tacky. Real tacky. Whoop. Just got one of Santa's legs. Hey, Dad. Lemme back at Santa. I wasn't through there.

"Fine. Fine. I wasn't finished here in the living room

anyway. Lamp. Have I knocked over the lamp yet today? Don't believe so. Lamp, lamp, lamp. Up we go. Onto the knees. On up to a full stand. Hey, nice view up here. Whoa! There goes the lamp. And that shade looks like good chewing.

"Hey, Old Man. It's just a lamp. Don't get so worked up. What do you mean how did I get there? Behind the chair, back by the radiator—the usual way. If you weren't so darn big, you could get around to some neat places, too.

"Wait a minute. Where the heck . . . My room? Oh, I get it. Nap time. I could use some rest. A guy gets tired doing all this decorating.

"Look, Dad. I'll be glad to sleep a while, but do me a favor, huh? Don't be rearranging everything while I'm sleeping. It was just starting to look good.

"Now, where's the smooth edge of this blanket?"

Let's get rolling

Took my son for a stroll the other day. Literally. He rode in the stroller. I pushed.

The system seems to be highly acceptable to both of us. He likes to ride. I like to walk.

It wasn't hard to tell the one-year-old was ready to go outside. Whenever he gets the urge to go out, he'll waddle over to you, wherever you happen to be.

He'll grab your index finger and start tugging. If you rise to your feet, he'll then lead you to the back door. He'll wave his arm at the door a couple of times.

"Outside?" you ask.

A smile parts his chubby little cheeks.

He would, I think, live outside. He would rather be there than anyplace else, except in his high chair when it's time to stoke more calories. He leads us to the back door several times a day. He cries when we come back to the house after strolls, backpack jaunts, or wagon rides. He doesn't want to come in.

I would like to claim that heredity is responsible, in part, for his affinity for the outdoors. I doubt it. I think it has a lot more to do with the fact that a one-year-old's main purpose in life is to explore, and let's face it—he's explored about all of the living room, dining room, and kitchen that he can.

So, the other day we strolled. We strolled the regular neighborhood route, past Bear, the neighbor's dog, then up the side street, down to the Community Center, and back home.

At intervals, my lumpy passenger would burst out laughing. He would cast a sideways glance at some house and just let out a big ol' guffaw. What was going on in that little mind? Did he see something he thought was funny, or was he merely vocalizing his pleasure with the goodness of life at that moment?

For long stretches, he would be silent. Every now and then, I'd stop and walk around front to see if he was awake. He'd stare at me with that round little face and a deadpan look that seemed to say, "Hey, Old Man, what are we stopping here for? Let's get rolling."

And we would get rolling again.

A stroll, in Duluth, in early April, is not without difficulties. The difficulties have nothing to do with the passenger. They have to do with potholes, puddles that must be forded and gravel that gets stuck in the front wheels of the stroller. We would be bumping along on a winter's worth of sand in the street when—lurch—suddenly, we'd be zagging sideways. I'd stop, work the stroller back and forth until the offending pebble was jarred loose, and we'd continue on our way.

Such minor problems are of no concern to a one-year-old. The only problem you can get into with a one-year-old is if you happen to stop and visit with a neighbor. A one-year-old wants action. He is bored by neighborly talk. Hold him motionless for more than thirty seconds, and he'll be squirming and moaning for a return to movement. Nearly always, he gets it.

The most serious problem you run into hauling a one-year-old around is women.

Most women love babies. Fat, cherubic, teeth-coming-in babies. Cute babies. Homely babies. Hairless babies. Drooling babies. You walk into an office with a baby in your arms or on your back, and the next thing you know, you're surrounded by cooing women. Works every time.

I believe you could walk through an office with triplets sprouting from a backpack and most men would walk past, look you in the eye, and say, "Morning, J. R."

Of course, not all men ignore babies. Not all women fawn over them. But grab a baby and conduct the experiment for yourself. You'll see.

We experienced no such problems on our stroll the other day. We saw some dogs. We saw some kids playing. We saw a pulp truck and its giant claw loading some brush.

Fascinating stuff for a one-year-old. Good for several hearty laughs and some extended jabbering.

Good for a dad, too. Makes a dad think about his own parents, and how many bumpy streets they must have wheeled him around more than forty years ago. Makes a dad think about the big circle of life, about giving and receiving.

That's what it was like on our stroll the other day, in the gravel and the puddles, watching the logging truck, laughing at houses.

Marilyn's house

All the regulars are there.

Brett.

Mikey.

Andrea.

Maren.

The red-headed baby whose name I forget.

Sam the dog.

They are bouncing around the room, rolling around in wheeled walkers, sitting in a playpen, hanging on to one of Marilyn's legs, peppering her with knee-high questions.

Day care.

A Tuesday morning.

They are all happy to see the little guy I'm dropping off. Andrea wonders if his older sister will be coming by after school.

She will.

It's a familiar scene, repeated hundreds of times each morning across our little city on the shores of Lake Superior.

Some of us who do it are two-parent families in which both parents want to work. Some of us are single-parent families in which there is little choice.

For our family, it's a part-time thing—one of us working full-time, the other half-time.

But there's no half-time for the two-year-old on the days we both work. He doesn't understand that tomorrow his mom will be able to stay home with him. He knows only that he can't loll around the living room in his pajamas with the feet in them until midmorning, playing trucks. He is dressed and combed and packed off to Marilyn's.

If you detect a note of wistfulness about all of this, your intuition is on the mark.

Understand, we couldn't have a better day-care mom than Marilyn. She loves her brood of dropped-off munchkins as much as any mom could—not the way she loves the six kids she raised herself, maybe, but a brand of love the kids know and trust and count on.

Her countenance rarely changes. I have seen her be firm with the kids but never mad. She has patience I envy. She feeds those kids, reads to them, helps us potty-train them, puts them down for naps, helps them make things their parents marvel at, and fills the backyard swimming pool for them. She has been known to come to their birthday parties.

They love her, I think, as much as any child can love someone who is not his or her parent.

And still, I wonder if it's the right thing to do.

I have heard all the rationalizations.

"It's good for them to be around other kids."

"They won't be spoiled."

"They have to learn how to get along with others."

All of which is true.

But some days, when the little fellow wraps his arms around my neck and his legs around my waist and doesn't want to let go, or when the tears come and Marilyn has to help pry his body off mine, I can't help wondering if this is the way things should be.

I drive to work on those days trying to feel right about it and never quite succeeding. I am only partially comforted when, at day's end, I go by to pick him up and he doesn't want to quit playing to come home.

Today it is going to be easy. My little partner trots over to greet Marilyn. He has a question for her, about a rake he saw on the porch. He gets his answer, comes back for a quick hug, and is off to play.

I leave feeling reasonably sure that all is well, that this choice we have made is the right one—that we have struck some kind of balance between money and time and love.

I hope so.

Tuned in

OK.

I'll be right up front about it.

I'm a World Series junkie.

It's a sickness, an affliction, a malady, an annual curse. And I love it.

I watch little television the rest of the year, but when the baseball playoffs and World Series come around, I budget up to forty-two hours (fourteen three-hour games) to sit spellbound before the TV. Budget, heck—those hours just sort of vanish from the rest of my life while I assume the activity of a large turnip.

I'm sure I'm not the only one suffering from this delicious disease. I know a lot of casual baseball fans who become riveted to the playoffs and World Series. People like me who couldn't write out a lineup card for the Minnesota Twins in June are now second-guessing Twins manager Tom Kelly for batting Al Newman in place of Mike Pagliarulo late in the game.

Part of it for us forty-somethings goes back to junior high school. That's when most of us lived with Rawlings mitts dangling from one hand, and we still believed there was a decent chance we could make it in the big leagues. Series games were played during the days, not evenings, back in the sixties.

To keep abreast of the action, we'd race to transistor radios at our teachers' desks between classes.

The really cool guys had an even better method. They'd steal a thick book from their parents, then cut a deep square in the center of its pages.

That's where the mini-radio would go. The earphone cord would run out between the pages, up a sleeve to the earphone in the cool guy's ear. He'd be sitting there in geography, ostensibly trying to recall the capital of North Dakota, when suddenly he'd start convulsing in his seat, pounding on his desk and blurt out, "Mantle just hit one out!"

Which, having nothing to do with North Dakota, usually resulted in a radio confiscation by Mr. Monnington.

Now, with baseball in prime time, the challenges are a little different. It is difficult, for instance, to be an involved husband and father while mesmerized by the green and blue glow in the corner of the room. I mean, when your seven-year-old says, "Mom, what's that growing on the couch?" and you hear, somewhere far beneath the din of the Metrodome crowd, a voice something like that of your wife saying, "Why, honey, that's your father," it almost gives you a twinge of guilt.

Almost.

So far, the best viewing this fall occurred one night during the National League playoffs on one of those rare warm October nights in Duluth. I went over to watch a few innings with a friend, who had moved his television outside onto his deck. We sat there on patio furniture, under a half moon, in light jackets, reveling in the ballgame.

At home, though, I've found you can still be semiproductive while watching baseball. You can wash dishes between innings. You can put another load of laundry in the washer and bring up a dry load from the dryer. You can even fold towels between pitches.

The problem comes when the Twins are starting to rally at the same time you have to put your twenty-month-old down to sleep.

That calls for creative parenting. And a good radio. What I do is put the radio up on my son's dresser. Right along side the horsey lamp and the teddy bear. I turn the radio down to where I can just hear the Twins announcers, Herb Carneal and John Gordon. Then we sing some nighty-night songs and rock in the rocking chair.

Me: Twinkle, twinkle, little star . . .

Herb Carneal: The pitch from Timlin . . .

Me: How I wonder what you are.

Carneal: Outside, ball two.

Me: Up above the world so high, like a diamond in the . . .

Carneal: Pagliarulo hits a long drive! White goes back, back. It's a home run!!

Me: SKY!!!

Which sort of shatters the lullaby mood.

But contrary to what my wife might tell you, I did not throw the boy up in the air. And if I had, I'd have just tapped my mitt a couple of times and caught him to retire the side.

Night of the sick child

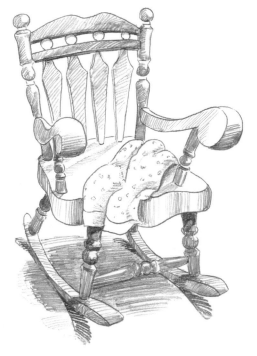

We wheeled into the driveway at a quarter till 2:00.

A quarter till 2:00 A.M.

You know, as parents of two young whippersnappers, that morning is going to come early after a night like that.

The whippersnappers had been left at home with a baby–sitter, but I've always said that if you're going to stay out that late at night you need two baby–sitters—one at night, one for the next morning.

Otherwise, you wake up feeling as if maybe the national Boy Scout Jamboree has been held on your body. There's a two-year-old climbing all over you with his blanket in tow, and he's saying, "Ready to eat, Dad."

Those were the kinds of thoughts going through my mind when we pulled into the drive that Saturday morning at 1:45. Then my wife and I looked in the kitchen window and saw the baby–sitter lunging for the kitchen sink with the two-year-old in her arms.

Figuring it wasn't likely the baby–sitter was doing that just so the child could get a better look at the drain, we hustled into the house. Of course. He was sick.

A lot of things go trotting through your mind at a point like that. You feel sorry for the child. You feel sorry for the baby–sitter who has had to deal with the sick kid. You feel sorry for the baby–sitter's mother, whom the baby–sitter called—wisely—for backup support in our absence and who was pulling in the drive at that moment.

You also know the four or five hours of sleep you had hoped to get is now going to be run through the sleep Cuisinart and spit out at you and your spouse in small pieces. It's an ugly prospect, but one for which there's no alternative. That little guy needs all the support you can muster, and you're going to give it to him.

We paid the baby–sitter. We thanked her mother. We got the little guy into some clean jammies.

Then we went to bed and waited for the Night of the Sick Child to unfold.

Now, I strongly dislike having my sleep messed with. When it comes to bouncing out of bed prematurely to nurture a sick wife or a sick child, and sometimes even to go fishing, I'm a wimp.

Sitting there on the edge of the bed, my brain feels like it's made from yesterday morning's oatmeal scrapings. My legs feel skinny and cold. My mouth tastes as if little people have been shoving kerosene-soaked cottonballs into it while I snored.

I hate that.

But there was a small person in the next room who my wife and I decided to bring onto the planet, and he needed us, and he needed us at that moment. So, we went. At 3:30 A.M. and 4:19 A.M. and 5:41 A.M.

We would do whatever needed to be done each time. We'd take the limp little lump out of his crib and feel for a rise in temperature and hustle him off to the bathroom or squirt some Tempra between his lips or rock him until the coughing spell passed.

Once I was up, I felt a strange sense of satisfaction in all of that. I have felt the same way on canoe trips, when late in the day you realize you and your partner aren't going to find a camp where you expected to. You realize you have another three or four miles to paddle, and maybe a portage or two to make. You might stop for a hit of raisins or a candy bar. Then you grab that paddle and do what needs to be done.

In some way, paddling and parenting aren't so different.

Having a partner to share the load with is part of it.

But the larger part is sitting there in the rocking chair with that twenty-five-pound bundle burrowed into your chest, knowing that he needs you, knowing that you're doing everything you can for him.

In a very simple way, you are doing one of the most important things you can do in this short little trip called life.

There will be other nights to sleep.

Letting go

We are in the grocery store. My seven-year-old wants to know if she can go get a drink. The drinking fountain is six aisles away.

"No," I tell her.

We are at home. Our seven-year-old wants to ride her bike to a friend's house. The house is a block and a half away. Around a corner. Along a wooded street. We tell her we will walk halfway with her and watch her ride the rest of the way.

We know friends of hers, seven- and eight-year-olds, who ride all over. Across a four-lane street. Down to the convenience store. Around the neighborhood.

We deliberate almost daily, my wife and I, about how much to let go. We want our daughter to feel free, to become more and more independent, to know the heady feeling that comes with expanding her boundaries.

We live in a relatively safe community. This is Duluth. This isn't Detroit or Washington, D.C., or even Minneapolis.

But it's also 1991, and we are aware of the realities of the world. We cannot put out of our minds the story of Jacob Wetterling's disappearance from St. Joseph and other stories like it.

Our seven-year-old wants to know why she can't roam as far as some of her friends. We try to tell her. She knows about Jacob Wetterling. She knows about some of the other bad things that have happened to good people.

She looks at the pictures in the newspaper that arrives each morning. She wants to know what has happened. We try to tell her the truth, translating it into language that will make sense to a seven-year-old mind, tempering it with the reassurance that those kinds of things aren't likely to happen in our neighborhood, or in our town.

We want to believe that, too.

We talk about this issue with other parents. We want to know what they think. Are we the only ones wondering if we're overprotective with our kids? When is a child old enough to ride two blocks on her own? Or four blocks? Or down to the convenience store?

I'm not sure.

We think we're doing the right thing. I'm sure parents who give their children a freer rein believe they're doing the right thing, too. Maybe it doesn't make a big difference.

All I know is how I feel in a shopping center or at a store or on the street when my child gets out of my sight for a few minutes. Minutes, heck. Seconds. If I can't look around the corner of an aisle or down a hall and see her—well, I suspect if you're a parent you know the feeling that grips you.

I know what the odds are of something bad happening. Slim. Almost nil. My head knows that. My gut still tells me not to let my girl go roving across the supermarket for a drink of water while I choose cereals. I can't do it.

What makes me think I'll be more willing to let my girl ride a few blocks to a friend's house at nine years old than I am when she's seven? Will she be safer then? A stronger bike rider? Less apt to talk to a stranger in a car? Less vulnerable to someone who would represent a threat to her?

I don't know. I'll deal with that when she is nine.

Would I feel differently if my seven-year-old were a boy rather than a girl? I don't think so. A kid is a kid.

The hardest part in all of this is having to make our girl aware of why we put these limits in place, why we choose to say "no" sometimes. I don't mind saying "no" to candy or pop or sleep-overs when it seems the right thing to do. But I dislike having to make my daughter aware of the unpleasant realities of our world. A seven-year-old shouldn't have to carry around the burden of good touch and bad touch, of strangers in cars, of people with guns.

But that's part of what it means to be seven in 1991, even in Minnesota, even in Duluth. Mostly, it still means soccer and T-ball and playing house with friends. Mostly, it still means trusting and believing in grown-ups. Mostly, it still means thinking the world is a good place to live.

But, at least for now, if my girl needs a drink at the supermarket, I'll stop shopping and go with her.

Quality time

Hey, we consider it a success. Nobody fell into the campfire.

It was just the nine of us, paddling into the Boundary Waters Canoe Area Wilderness for a little solitude.

Two families. Four

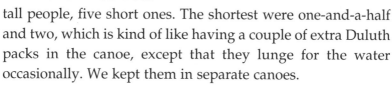

tall people, five short ones. The shortest were one-and-a-half and two, which is kind of like having a couple of extra Duluth packs in the canoe, except that they lunge for the water occasionally. We kept them in separate canoes.

We forged deep into the canoe country. At least a mile. We even passed up one campsite.

Possibly, wherever you were that weekend, you saw the shadow of one of our canoes passing. Some people thought it was a solar eclipse. One canoe, for instance, carried three portly Duluth packs, a daypack full of rain gear and cameras, the diaper bag, the baby backpack teetering atop the mountain of Duluth packs, and the loose plastic bag with the Wiffle ball, the bat, and the toy truck. All of which left plenty of room for Dad in the stern seat, the seven-year-old up front paddling, and Mom and the twenty-five-pounder corralled on the bottom of the canoe amidships.

It was a fine trip. Really. If you bring enough peanut butter and jelly and Cheerios, anything is possible. It wasn't so much that meals were the focus of the trip. It's just that one seemed to begin shortly after the other one ended. In the ten minutes or so between meals, the seven- to eleven-year-olds would play campsite baseball, pausing between innings to ask if there was any more Kool-Aid. Which there usually wasn't, if you didn't count the Purplesaurus Rex that had spilled into the raisins at breakfast.

But nighttime. That's the magical time.

What is it about tents and toddlers? Kids love tents. They must think a tent is a wonderful place, an architectural hybrid of a crib and the Hubert H. Humphrey Metrodome.

There are two ways to get an eighteen-month-old to sleep. One is to take him out to the fire, where you rock him until the fire and the stars mesmerize him. That takes about forty-five minutes. The other way is the Flop-Till-You-Drop technique, in which you let the small person bounce around the inside of the tent, flying from one sleeping bag to the next, until finally he can no longer get up. This, too, takes about forty-five minutes.

That first night was something. Hard to say what time it was when the small person, sleeping next to the seven-year-old, woke up wailing. The tent probably seemed more like the Metrodome than the crib then. Or maybe he was cold, because he had migrated out of his sleeping bag. Mom took the first shift, trying to rock the boy back to sleep while the rest of us listened to his protests. I am not talking only about the people in our tent.

Half an hour later, Mom said to Dad, "Take him outside and walk him." Being the sensitive nineties kind of dad I am, I began groping for my glasses, socks, pants, shoes, and wool shirt. No problem. The boy and I would have some quality time together in the woods.

Have you ever tried to walk in the woods at night carrying, say, a twenty-five-pound sack of dog food on your chest, trying to keep its blankets from sliding off?

We staggered around for most of forty minutes, or maybe it was forty hours. Neither of us was wearing a watch. We tripped over logs. We walked through boughs of balsam fir. We stumbled over roots.

It's a jungle out there.

We were walking down near the canoes when I thought I finally had him almost asleep. Then, out from under the corner of a blanket, I heard him say, as if it were noon: "Boat!"

We walked until my arm was trembling too much to hold the little critter any longer; then we went back to the tent. Back to Mom, on whose tummy he writhed for a while longer.

It was sometime during that final writhing, replete with cries of frustration, that the seven-year-old's voice came soft and questioning from her Quallofil cocoon.

"When is it going to be morning?" she asked. "It seems like it's been a long night."

But like I said, nobody fell into the fire.

Gerbils and other realities of the forties

Words for rent

I called my friend Larry the other day.

"Larry," I said. "I need to put down a concrete run for my dog kennel. Is that something I can do myself?"

Larry knows me. Knows my skills with saw and square and level.

No, Larry said. I should not attempt to pour myself a dog run.

So, as always, I called around until I found someone who had the skills necessary to do the job, asked him what it would cost, and paid him to do it.

He came a couple of weeks ago. Did it in one day. Now I have a nice dog run.

Which is not the point.

The point is that it would be nice, once in a while, to barter for services like making a dog run instead of shelling out two-thirds of a week's take-home pay. But let's face it. I'm just lucky to be living in the 1990s, where a guy can eke out a living tapping keys on a keyboard and inventing sentences that weren't there before. If I had to make a living actually doing something—making something that other people needed—I'd be out of luck.

At times, I have toyed with the idea of trying to barter my skills as a wordsmith.

Take Rick, the guy who did my dog run.

"Hey Rick," I could have said. "How 'bout you pour my dog run and I'll do some writing for you. Need any writing done around home? I could write something about your kids. We could have it laminated."

See what I mean? It won't work.

I needed some dead birches cut down a couple of years ago. Rather than dropping the trees on my house, I had a guy do it for me. Maybe I should have tried to work a deal with him.

"Hey, buddy. How about you cut my trees down, and I write a letter to your mother for you. It would be nice. When did you write her last, anyway? You could sign it, and she'd really appreciate it. Or I could write one a month to her for three months. Fair enough?"

No.

It isn't going to fly.

What people want is hard labor. Pianos moved. Porches painted. Houses wired.

I have lots of friends who trade labor with each other. Bob helps Jim build a garage. Jim helps Bob sheetrock a rec room.

Nobody ever asks me to help them do anything. I think I know why. They're afraid I'd do it. I'd show up with my virgin tape measure on my belt and an eager expression on my face, and my friend would immediately know what he had on his hands. Another kid. At best, I could hand him the things he needed.

It hasn't always been this way. I was, for a period of years, fairly good help when I was young and in farm country. Oh, I did yank out a bit of Roger Aberle's barbed-wire fence when I swung too wide on a corner with a big John Deere and a rotary hoe one day. But Roger seemed to understand.

Mostly, I was a ninety-five-pound kid wrestling seventy-pound bales of hay in barns that felt like saunas. I wasn't going to mess anything up too badly. I worked hard. I got paid a fair wage.

But then I went to college, learned to write, and lost all hope of trading my skills for actual work. All my words are worth now is money. Don't get me wrong. I like the money.

It just seems like a dog run is worth a lot more than, say, this story.

Hey, Rick. When was the last time you surprised your wife with a truly romantic poem? Huh? Think about it, pal. What that would mean to her. How she'd love you for it.

I'll get started on it in the morning.

More than a game

I was listening to a Minnesota Twins game on the radio the other night, and I got to wondering. Do you think Kirby Puckett chatters?

You know what I mean. Baseball chatter.

"Hum, babe. Throw him the dark apple. Rock 'n' fire, babe. Put it by him. No stick. You got him, babe. Attababe."

I spent a large portion of my childhood standing on a sandy playground in a pair of blue jeans and a T-shirt uttering that mantra.

"Talk to me, now. Say you will, babe. Bring him the heat. Hum, babe. Hum, babe."

And I wonder, does a guy making $5 million a year still talk like that?

You know what I think? Yes.

Partly because Kirby is Kirby. And partly because baseball is baseball. I feel I have a good insight into these things. Kirby and I have a fair amount in common, after all.

No, not salary.

But I'm sure Kirby grew up believing he was going to be a big-league baseball player. So did I.

Baseball wasn't just a game to play. It wasn't just something to do between mowing the lawn and going swimming. Baseball was a way of life.

We'd get up in the morning, wolf down some Corn Flakes, and head for the Wasmer Elementary School playground. Nobody ever called to see if we were playing. We just showed up. There was always a game.

We chose sides and went at it.

A lot of what we learned about being boys—or men—we learned on the baseball diamond. We learned to negotiate while arguing over close plays on the basepaths. We learned to play with pain—jammed fingers, sore arms, and scabbed hips. We learned to win and lose.

I'm not saying those were the best principles we could have acquired to carry us through life, but that's the way it was. We were boys in the fifties. We played ball.

Our most important possessions were our gloves and bats and balls. Each winter, when baseball season finally ended, I would put my ball in my glove and put the glove under my mattress. All winter, as I slept, I was forming an ever more perfect pocket in my mitt.

This was in Nebraska, and when tornado warnings sounded in the summer, I'd grab my mitt before I'd head to the basement to wait out the storm. It was the one possession I couldn't imagine being without.

A good bat—a Louisville Slugger, of course—was something to be cherished. We each had our favorites—thick-handled Nelson Foxes, thin-gripped Mickey Mantles.

And did we wear out some baseballs. There was nothing like the gritty sand and the fine gravel of a schoolyard to rough up the hide of a ball. We had no such thing as a new ball, at least not for more than a morning. My memory of baseballs is that they were brown. When they got wet, we would beg our moms to dry them out in the oven on low heat.

I don't know how old I was when I realized that I wouldn't be moving up to the big leagues. It may have been when I was a freshman in high school in Omaha, and I got cut from the baseball team.

It hurt a lot. But by then I had begun to see other paths in life. Girls, for one. And fishing. Not that I could see much professional opportunity in either of those, but at least I wasn't going to be bored.

But I do not regret holding for so many years the dream of being a ballplayer. There are still few pursuits in life that bring more pure satisfaction than tracking down a long fly ball to left-center, although the last time I tried it I pulled a hamstring pretty badly. It seemed a small price to pay for having something in common with Kirby Puckett.

Hum, babe.

Groovin'

At 8:45 on a Saturday night, I would appear to be piloting the family station wagon along I-35 as it snakes through the Twin Cities.

But no. I'm groovin'.

I'm behind the wheel of the car, all right, but I'm tuned to a classic rock radio station.

I've got Wayne Fontana and the Mindbenders blaring "The Purpose of a Man Is to Love a Woman," and most of me has been transported back to Mike Estle's 1956 Ford Fairlane. It is 11:00 P.M. on a 1965 October night in rural Kansas. Another night of high school play practice is behind us, and the rest of our lives are ahead of us.

Here in 1989, the full moon is rising over the St. Paul skyline. But to me all those buildings look like fence posts and cornstalks, and the moon is coming up over the Kansas farm country. It is Mike and I, and maybe Lynette Judah or Connie Minton or Anita Mishler in the car. It doesn't matter precisely who it is, and we aren't traveling those back roads to steal kisses or fall in love. We just ride around as long as we can, listening to the radio, reveling in the sweet glory of being alive and sixteen.

Now the radio station sends me the Beatles, cranking out "Sergeant Pepper's Lonely Hearts Club Band," and I'm rubber-banded immediately to Dick Olsson's room in the fraternity house, where the stereo is cranking and Olsson is juggling two pop bottles and a butcher knife. It is 1967 or '68 and I'm a wide-eyed freshman or sophomore at the University of Kansas.

I'm in for a wonderful night, alone in the station wagon. The cruise control is set at 65—OK, 66—and I'm northbound for Duluth with this radio station that is replaying the 1960s and 1970s for me.

This is chic now, among radio stations—this "classic rock" programming for us baby boomers. I have heard it from Duluth to Minneapolis to Tampa, Florida. We are the significant generation, it seems, because there are so many of us and because advertisers want us to reach into our pocketbooks.

That is why, on a Saturday night in 1989, I can drive from Minneapolis to Duluth with nonstop nostalgia.

Alone, I beat the steering wheel and the dashboard. I flail my gas-pedal knee. And I sing.

I sing with volume and feeling and meaning—the kind of singing no high-school chorus teacher could ever elicit from me. I miss words here and there, but my backups—the Temptations, the Four Tops, Paul Revere and the Raiders—always bail me out.

We sound good, I think. Darn good.

Nothing yanks me back to those supercharged years of high school and college the way those old songs do. What was so intoxicating about that time of our lives that even now, twenty-five years later, I can recall most of the lyrics from the Beach Boys' "Help Me, Rhonda," yet I can't always remember to put the garbage cans out on Wednesdays?

Give me the right song, and a scene from one of those indelible years becomes so palpable, so real, it's as if it happened last week.

When the Beatles sing "All You Need Is Love," I'm at the

ballpark, watching Dave Frey, our centerfielder, lace up his spikes with the door of his 1965 Ford Galaxy swung open.

Play me the Byrd's version of "Mr. Tambourine Man," and there's Mark Hink, playing his guitar on the Persian rug in the fraternity house living room.

When I hear that haunting instrumental opening from the Mamas and the Papas' "California Dreamin'," I'm sitting in the dashlight glow of my old Ford with my high school sweetheart beside me after a basketball game.

I revisit all of those places—and twenty or thirty more—on my drive north.

As much as I love that music, I still don't try to understand it. What are, for instance, the "hippy, hippy shakes?" Is there deeper meaning to the phrase "Woolly Boolly" when Sam the Sham and the Pharaohs sing it?

Personally, I find it somewhat embarrassing that I imprinted on Mitch Ryder and the Detroit Wheels lyrics like *She's not too skinny/And she's not too fat/She's a real humdinger/And I like 'em like that.* But I did.

The music carries me past Sandstone and Moose Lake and Barnum, right over Thompson Hill into Duluth. I am flying. I don't want to turn off the radio and lose my umbilical link to the sixties. But I am, after all, a husband and father and normal eighties guy.

So, instead of driving around, I go home.

I am only moderately self-conscious when I get back in the car to take the fourteen-year-old baby-sitter home and realize the radio volume knob is still set on Blow-Your-Brains-Out. I turn it down and explain to the baby-sitter about my trip.

I say to her, "Someday, about twenty or thirty years from now, you'll be driving across the country somewhere, alone, listening to the music you love right now, and you'll understand what I'm talking about."

She nods and mumbles.

Which, as I recall, is how I always reacted when older geeks talked weird to me.

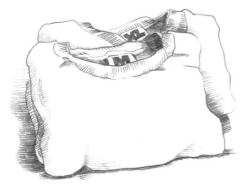

On becoming an XL guy

I am riding a personal high of late.

Feeling good. Feeling right. Feeling high on life.

I got myself some new underwear.

It fits.

Now, that may not seem like anything revolutionary to you, but trust me. This is something of a personal breakthrough for me.

This is not just a matter of undergarments. This is a matter of self-awareness, an acceptance of myself for what I am.

For years, I've been wearing T-shirts that weren't quite large enough. I always bought a size large.

I bought larges in spite of considering myself a medium sort of guy. I disperse roughly 155 pounds over a six-foot frame. Nobody has ever called me "big-boned" or "square-shouldered" or "well-muscled."

Still, I'd get these large-sized T-shirts home, wash them once, put them on and think someone had sprayed my torso with aluminum paint. They'd bind in the armpits. They'd cling to my chest, perma-pressing my seven chest hairs. The sleeves would cling tight against my weenie arms.

But I wore them. I'd paid good money for them, and I wasn't going to waste them. So, week in and week out, I'd walk around being scrinched to death. My torso was crying out for breathing room. My armpits were yearning to be free.

I tried to put on a good front. I'd smile. I'd be pleasant. But it was killing me.

To you, looking at this objectively, I suppose the answer would seem obvious—buy larger T-shirts.

I never could do that. An extra-large? Me? For years, I thought buying a large was living on the edge, flirting with unknown territory. I didn't consider myself a true large.

I think it goes back to my childhood, when I was a runt. I was always one of the wimpiest guys in my class at school. I barely met minimum physical standards for high-school graduation.

Oh, I was a whiz at the Shuttle Relay event in the Presidential Physical Fitness program. That was the one where you scampered back and forth on the gym floor snatching erasers like some crazed ferret. But when it came to real sports, I was— this is true—a goggle-eyed student manager. I didn't realize it then, but I know it now. I've peeked at the yearbooks. I was dangerously close to being a geek.

I grew late. I was well into college before my testosterone kicked in. I took the cardboard out of my razor and put in a blade. I put on a few pounds. I got taller. I sprouted my first two chest hairs.

The problem is, when you've been a runt so long, you can't be objective about your size. I had blossomed into this man-child thing, and yet in my mind I was still a student manager.

And, at forty-one, I was still wearing junior-high T-shirts.

All of that has changed now. Last week, my wife was headed out to do some shopping. I asked her to pick me up some T-shirts.

Yes. I'll say it.

Extra-larges.

She brought them home. Three of them. They felt as heavy as towels. I opened the package and unfolded them. They just kept unfolding.

I put one on. Sure, it hung almost to my knees, but it felt good.

I washed them. I dried them. I put one on.

A nice, comfortable fit at the neck. I looked down inside the front of it. My chest hairs were stretching luxuriously. I took a mental inventory of my armpits. No bindage. And my sleeves hung loosely around my arms.

Like I say, life couldn't be better now. Think about it. Me. An extra-large kind of guy.

Yeah. Don't push me, pip-squeak.

Weeding and feeding

I'll be honest. I've never been a turf man.

My idea of a yard is anything that grows between my neighbor's driveway and mine. Give me your tired broadleaf weeds, your poor henbit, your huddled chickweed yearning to breathe free. If they're green—any shade of green—they're good enough for me. I'll level them every week or so with the eighteen-year-old Lawn Boy and call it good.

Oh, I've got some real grass out there. It creeps in from my neighbors'yards. I can't keep it out. It's invading some of the areas where I have good stands of dandelions, hawkweed, and clover.

Which is to say, my yard looks partly like a yard and partly like a tossed salad. Then there are a few areas that appear to be victims of some funguslike problem. They're circular and dry looking, something like pictures of that rash that accompanies Lyme disease.

But, hey, those spots mow fast.

I had always been happy with that kind of yard. Then I heard my neighbor, Mel, talking about something called Weed and Feed. It's a weed killer and fertilizer, all in one. Mel has more than a yard. He has turf.

So, I decided it was time I became a turf man. I bought some Weed and Feed.

Weeding and feeding is not something you take lightly, I learned after reading the instructions.

You have your User Precautions, your Instructions, your Storage Directions, your Product Disposal Directions, your Container Disposal Directions, and your Environmental Hazards.

The instructions told me to (1) mow my lawn a day or two before applying my Weed and Feed, (2) water the lawn thoroughly at least one day before application, (3) apply the Weed and Feed when weeds are young and actively growing, preferably in the morning when dew is on the grass, and (4) do not wash Weed and Feed from weeds for one to two days, then water thoroughly.

Right. I didn't buy fertilizer. I bought a new lifestyle.

Then, not far from the instructions, was the kicker.

"It is a violation of federal law to use this product in a manner inconsistent with its labeling."

That's why you've been seeing those U.S. marshals cruising your neighborhood. They're not looking for escaped criminals. They're making sure there's dew on the grass when you're weeding and feeding.

So, when dew came, I wed and fed.

Then, just to be sure the marshals couldn't find me, I took my family and headed to the woods for a few days. We could always elude them in Canada, I figured.

It was as if the weather gods had read my Weed and Feed instructions. Two days, no rain. Then, big rain. We came home.

I no longer had a lawn. I had turf—about three patches of it. They were surrounded by large swatches of wilted weeds. My dandelions hung their heads. None of my clover was lucky. My henbit had bitten the dust.

The yard looked like a salad bar left out in the sun too long.

I thought a mowing might help, but mowing was no longer fun. It used to be those weeds stood tall and proud, and it was fun whacking them down to size. Now the dandelions lay sprawled and withered, too low to become candidates for my blade.

I felt like a lone lieutenant, patrolling a battlefield at dawn the day after a big battle.

There is hope, I figure. The Weed and Feed instructions say "possible retreatment may be necessary."

No way. If my weeds can bounce back on their own, why, I say they deserve to live. I see a yard green and yellow and off-green. I see grass. I see broadleaves. I see stems of varying height and thickness.

I see life.

I do not see me becoming a turf man.

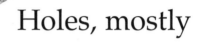

Holes, mostly

Someday, maybe, I'll live in a house where the doorknobs don't fall off.

It happened again the other day. I grabbed the bathroom doorknob, turned it and—*voop*—I was left standing in a hallway with a doorknob in my hand.

The door didn't move.

This happens regularly for two reasons:

1. I live in a 1904 home.

2. I am do-it-yourself impaired.

I grew up in a home where there was no such thing as a toolbox or a workbench. All we had were a pair of pliers and a screwdriver.

That was it. Our tool kit.

I never saw my dad or mom fix anything. They are good people. They just never had—and consequently couldn't pass on—the genes necessary to run a tool more complex than a sanding block.

So, at middle age, when I am at the peak of my earning power and should be enjoying the fruits of life, I sit in the bathtub and stare at the steel nub of a doorknob shaft.

I have tried to get handy. About three years ago I went to buy a drill. You know, a drill that plugs in. I'd just heard about them.

I will admit I am intimidated by these macho hardware men in red vests whose world is defined by semi-paste flux, screw eyes, and toggle switches. I swear these guys have Stanley tape measures implanted in their abdominal skin so that when they put on their pajamas at night, they can measure things if they need to.

"So, what will you be using your drill for?" the hardware guy asked me.

"Holes, mostly," I told him.

What did he think? Did he think I might be using a one-sixteenth-inch carbon steel bit to fill my own cavities? All I knew about drills was that you put bits in them and made holes in things. I had no plans for my drill. I had no projects waiting in the works. I had no specific hole sizes in mind.

I just wanted a drill. It was a statement more than anything else. I was ready to get handy.

Well, I got a drill.

It has led to other things. I feel as if I am now in the adolescence of being a handyman. Sort of a handyboy, I guess you'd say.

I drill holes. I screw in screws. I remove flaking paint. All with my drill and its various attachments.

No longer do I tiptoe into the hardware store with that plaintive look in my eyes. I swagger. I swagger because I have discovered the way to get respect from the macho hardware store guys.

Wear a tape measure on your belt.

I don't care if you're stopping by after church on Sunday in your gray flannel suit. If you've got a tape measure on your belt, it tells the hardware store guy, "This customer knows his molly anchors from his strap hinges."

113

Which brings up the main problem with being handy: the vocabulary. Who's in charge of thinking up the names for this stuff?

You've got your clevis pins, lag bolts, and wood shims. You've got wire nuts, hitch pin clips, and galvanized deck zippers. Do you need a sillcock handle? How about a three-eighth-inch drill chuck? Doesn't your shop need a spoke shave, a chamfer bit, and a forty-five-degree street ell?

I am a hardware illiterate. Every time I go to the store, it's a game of charades. I start making motions in the air and say something like, "Have you got one of those rubber things that looks sort of like a pear that hangs on a chain in your toilet and when you flip the flush handle it raises up and water goes out?"

"You mean a ballcock kit," the man in the vest says.

"Yeah, I think so," I say. "Let me see one."

We go to the ballcock kit aisle. Of course, that's what I need. I act cool.

"Yip," I say. "I think that'll do it. But let me double-check."

So, I whip out my Stanley tape measure and size up the shrink-wrapped ballcock package. I take it.

I go home, get out my drill for moral support, replace the ballcock system, and watch with amazement when the new one works.

Full of pride, I try to leave the bathroom to crow about my success. And the doorknob comes off in my hand again.

Humility. It's so easy to cultivate when you're merely a handyboy.

Hello, Dolly

I'm getting a little bit scared. I'm not even sure I should be going public with this. I'm doing so only with the hope that if others are suffering from the same affliction, they will take some comfort in knowing they're not alone.

I think I'm beginning to like country music.

It began almost without my noticing it. One of my hunting buddies, when we were out in western Minnesota hunting pheasants, would slip some Dolly Parton or some Emmylou Harris on his tape deck while we traveled between pieces of pheasant cover.

I let him know right away I disapproved of his taste, but he just laughed. Little did I know what was happening to me.

Last year, I noticed he began slipping in a Randy Travis here and there. Hard-core country.

Not long ago, I accidentally tuned my car radio to a country station—and left it there. Out of curiosity, I guess. Now I've made a complete road trip listening to almost nothing but country music.

I'm getting to where I know some of the country music stars. Not personally, understand, but by the sounds of their voices. They're an interesting group, those country folks. I've never known any other collection of individuals who've had so much to be unhappy about.

They are mostly unhappy because they're going to lose their man or their woman, depending upon the gender of the singer, and that usually involves another man or another woman. Or they've just lost their man or woman. If the singers aren't sad about it, they're mad about it. Or they're just jealous and living with it.

I used to think that people who enjoyed country music must get extremely depressed listening to the twang and hurt in all those songs, but I've changed my mind on that theory. You listen to eight or ten of those down-and-out stories and suddenly your problems don't seem half as bad. You listen to a couple of hours of that stuff and you're on top of the world again.

You think, hey, I don't have it made, but at least I ain't that bad off.

That's another thing that happens—you start thinking in country music words. You can't help it. No more do you suspect your wife is going out on you. She's cheatin'. You aren't just a little depressed. You're hurtin'. Country singers don't mince words.

One thing I can't figure out is where these country stars get their names. Do they have these names from birth, or is there some factory in Nashville where all up-and-coming country singers get renamed and fitted for one of those white cowboy hats? You can't have a normal name, like Jason or Ryan or Steve, and be a country singer. The only kind of man's name that qualifies is the kind you'd see engraved in the back of a wide leather belt. Like Waylon. Or Garth. Or Clint. Or Randy.

You ever seen a cowboy walkin' around with the name Elton carved in his belt? I didn't think so.

And if you want to be a woman country star, you have to be a Dottie or a Dolly or an Emmylou or a Tanya or a Patsy. Near as I can tell, there are no female country singers named Mary or Martha or Gladys. And there sure as heck aren't any Pips singing in the background.

But what I like about the music—and the people who write it—is its honesty. When you've had a long day of listening to recorded voice mail messages and corporate business-speak, you get in your rig, crank up some country, and tune into some real talk.

"Pardon me, you left your tears on the jukebox/And I believe they got mixed up with mine."

"Let's tie our love in a double-knot."

"I may be worn, but I'm not worn out/I may be used, but I'm not used up."

They have a knack for mixing the tangible with the intangible. It's no stretch for a country artist to weave something about an eighteen-wheeler's transmission into the same line with a love gone bad. The lyrics are full of wedding rings, cars, pawnshops, barstools, and jukeboxes.

And you don't need a detective to find the beat in a country song.

Don't get me wrong. Nothing will ever take the place of sixties music. That was the music that pulsed in my veins when my hormones were running roughshod over reason in my brain. That is real music.

But, dang.

There's something about the way Dolly's voice sort of quavers that I cain't get outta my head.

Too much me

I saw them again the other night.

They're these little things that have come to live with me. I was changing clothes and paused midchange to glance at the mirror. There they were. One on each side. Riding just above the area I consider my waist.

Little lumps of surplus me.

Dang.

Where did those things come from?

Here I am, a normal sort of guy trying to avoid a midlife crisis and ear hair, and I've got these little hip pads smiling at me from the mirror.

They came to live with me sometime during the past two years. It looks like someone parted my skin and inserted a couple of gerbils on each side. Now they live in there. Every now and then, the gerbils laugh and my little pouches jiggle.

I don't consider this funny.

I can't figure it out. I've always been a little lean, bordering on being a runt. I can remember hitting milestone weights as I grew up. I think I hit eighty when I was about a freshman in high school. I barely cleared one hundred before I graduated. I was six-feet tall before my body blossomed to its fulsome 155.

I've been at 157 for about as long as I can remember. I was 157 before the gerbils. I'm 157 now.

So, what's the deal? Are these gerbils weightless? Or are they using tiny tubes that connect to other parts of my body, sucking weight from those parts to sustain their rodenty little life in Hipland?

When I first saw this amplitude happening, I denied it.

Nope. Couldn't be. Must just be the angle I was looking at them from. Or the light.

Two years of this, however, in numerous light conditions and from many angles, have persuaded me that yes, it's true. This is not an apparition. That is me. All me.

The rest of me still looks as if it were made mostly of leftover spaghetti noodles and pipe cleaners. My shoulders look like something from a wiring diagram. My biceps, from years of pounding a word processor, resemble bicycle innertubes.

But right there at the equator, life is full and rich and flourishing.

And I'm mad as heck.

I run. I ride my bike. I do sit-ups. The rest of my body responds. It hums like a finely tuned network of spaghetti noodles and pipe cleaners.

But the gerbils still chuckle and my equator quakes.

I know how some guys solve this problem. They go to a surgeon, and the surgeon goes in after whatever's there. This will not happen to me. I'm not going to let anyone near me with a fillet knife.

I am also not going to buy any weight-loss plans. Those are for radio announcers.

And I'm not going to drink chocolate malts with funny names instead of eating breakfast and lunch. If the Big Cahuna in the Sky wanted us to drink those things, he wouldn't have let Dairy Queen create Blizzards.

I don't know exactly what I'm going to do.

Yes, I do.

I'm going to start a support group of us fortyish guys with this problem.

LUMPS, we'll call our group. Losing Unwanted Midriff Plumpitude Sensibly.

What we'll do is we'll get these little plastic exercise wheels and have them surgically implanted. Yep. Right in there with the gerbils.

A couple of weeks on those workout wheels and those gerbils will be skin and bones. And you'll see some guys walking around who look like they're made from twisted bands of steel.

That'll be us. Former LUMPS.

Look for us on the beach, baby.

Life as we know it

Thin mint binge

Today's topic is "How to Eat an Entire Row of Girl Scout Thin Mints and Still Feel Good about Yourself."

Yes, it can be done. I know. I did it just the other day.

OK. It wasn't an entire row. The packet had been opened, and I'm guessing that one, maybe two Thin Mints already had been eaten. I base my case on simple logic: Who would open a row of Thin Mints and not eat one?

Right. Nobody.

In case you're not living with a Brownie Girl Scout, as I am, then maybe I should describe Thin Mints. They are tiny discs, the very minimum size you could make a cookie and still call it a cookie. They're made mostly of air, with a texture resembling a frozen graham cracker, a light chocolate-mint taste, and a thin coating of chocolate.

A box of Thin Mints consists of two rows, each packaged in light cellophane. Each row must consist of fifteen or twenty individual cookies, but who's counting?

So, I was home alone the other day, eating a simple lunch. I was reading the latest issue of *In-Fisherman* magazine, which doesn't have much to do with the Thin Mints, except perhaps subliminally. Most of the copy in that magazine refers to fish that are lunkers, monsters, slabs, hawgs, or bucketmouths.

I'm not saying it was *In-Fisherman's* fault I kept putting Thin Mints in my bucketmouth, but you can see how it could contribute to the mood.

If you've ever eaten Thin Mints (and I'm guessing you have your secret little row-devouring stories of your own), you know the scenario. You innocently grab one, maybe two Thin Mints from that flimsy cellophane wrapper. You pop one in your mouth. It lies there on your tongue like some brown communion wafer for a couple seconds and—zip—it's gone.

You pop the second one, turning a page of *In-Fisherman* to reveal a deep-bellied walleye. One good crunch with your molars and the cookie is history.

A slight minty flavor swirls like mist in your mouth. It's a lovely sensation that deserves—no, demands—another Thin Mint.

Wait. Did I say one? I meant two. You wouldn't want to quit on an odd number.

So you reach blindly for the cellophane and separate a couple of Thin Mints from the row. Whoops. Did you see that? That ultralight cellophane ripped farther down into the cookies. Now you've got a problem. You can't very well seal the rest of the row when the cellophane is ripped.

Only one solution. You're going to have to eat the cookies down to the end of the rip. Actually, you'll have to take a couple past the end of the rip if you're going to get a good seal on the packet. So you do. You eat all of the cookies that got you down past the cellophane rip. This is nothing. We're talking a maximum of fifteen seconds per cookie—one bite, a couple of crunches, an inhalation of mint, and all that's left are some telltale crumbs at the corners of your lips.

Now, you look at the package again. Wouldn't you know it?

A few more Thin Mints have fallen forward. Yes, you could go to the effort of gingerly straightening them up, but chances are you'd rip that cellophane again, and you know what that means.

So, you eat the ones lying down. Three, maybe four.

OK.

That's really enough, you tell yourself.

But look at that package. What's left? Four measly cookies? You know if you leave those there, your wife and kids will say you hogged almost the whole row and just left those four as some token offering to be split among three other members of the household. Which would be true.

So, you have a choice. You're going to get grief either way— whether you eat the last four or leave them for the family to squabble over. You're a logical sort. If you're going to take the heat, you might as well get your money's worth.

You shake the last four cookies out, pop them like aspirin and toss the cellophane in the trash.

A row of Thin Mints, gone.

And, hey. Some Brownie gets to go horseback riding at Camp Roundelay this summer.

You have to feel good about that.

The selling game

Lurking in the recesses of my newspaper each Tuesday, Friday, and Sunday is the "Dateline" feature.

It's the item that allows regular human beings to make little real-estate ads of themselves in an effort to find a buyer, which is to say a lover, a mate, a husband, a wife, or someone to have an affair with.

Really.

I was reading "Dateline" for the first time the other day. Just recreationally, you understand.

The first thing I noticed is that you have to be familiar with "Dateline" language to understand the ads. They're full of code letters that make people sound more like government agencies— DBM, NSNA. Or days of the week—MWF. You have to know the codes to go shopping for the man or woman of your choice, or else you'll end up with merchandise you don't want.

SWF, for instance, means Single White Female. NSNA would be a Non-Smoking Native American. If you're looking for an SWF, you probably don't want to accidentally end up getting an MWM, which is a Married White Male.

You get the idea.

The ads usually run something like this:

"SWF, 32, attractive, outdoorsy, loves country music, seeks SWM 25–40 who is caring, likes to dance, and wants quality time for just the two of us. Write Box 9999."

You read a few of these ads, and you'd think the world is full of beautiful, mature, fun-loving, intimate, caring folks, most of whom like to dance.

Now that may be true. But I've seen enough real-estate ads and then seen the actual homes to know a little glossing-over goes on in those fine-print descriptions.

I say it's time for some honesty in these ads.

If I were going to advertise myself in "Dateline," well, sure, I could say something like:

"SWM, 43, Arnold Schwarzenegger build, superb athlete, excellent angler, introspective yet outgoing, seeks SWF 18–20, who loves to dance, enjoys long walks on the beach, taking risks, and intimacy."

Sure. I could.

I'm sure I'd be flooded with letters from SWFs.

But somewhere along the way, the truth is going to come out, and some poor SWF is going to realize the ad should have read:

"MWM, 43 going on 50, some settling of contents may have occurred during shipping, understands Paul Simon lyric 'Why am I so soft in the middle when the rest of my life is so hard?', last athletic act was throwing ball back over fence to two people playing tennis (took two tries), recalls dancing at high school prom and wedding, considers intimacy being in same room with woman while listening to Minnesota Twins game on radio (would need to turn up volume on big plays), would consider a big night on the town stopping for caramel corn at Canal Park (and, hey, *I buy*), home repair abilities limited to looking up number for plumber, slightly pigeon-toed, wears thick glasses, some high-frequency hearing loss, built like Olive Oyl, wore orthodontia but not long enough."

There.

Now, we're talking facts.

I might not get many SWFs to answer that ad, but you can bet the one that does is going to know what she's getting.

There's another whole breed of "Dateline" ads, and those are placed by people seeking a specific person.

"Would like to hear from person who sits in seat M13, Section B2, at Duluth Symphony."

Right.

I can see my ad for that kind of person.

"Would like to meet woman who was fishing off Arrowhead Fishing Pier two Saturdays ago. You know who you are. You were using a dead smelt on one line, a leech on the other, and you had four more leeches hanging from your lower lip, ready to use. I like that. Write BOX FISH."

But, of course, I wouldn't need to place that ad.

I'm a happy MWM, and I'm not in the market for an SLWFW.

Oh, an SLWFW?

That's a Single Leech-Wearing Fisher-Woman.

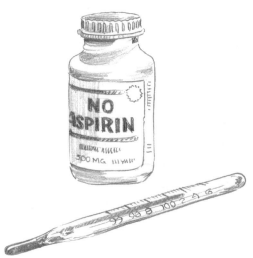

Fever dreams

I knew when I was starting to get sick. I was watching the cashier at the grocery store ring up a basketful of my groceries. The longer I looked at that stream of food passing before me, the more I had the feeling I'd been riding in the rear-facing seat of a station wagon on a winding road.

Dang.

I'd been smugly pleased that in spite of those falling sick around me, I had remained healthy. Now it was my turn.

I went home, unpacked the groceries, and crawled into bed. Funny, when the woman in the next cubicle at work tells you she feels sick, it's no big deal. But when *you're* sick, that's something else. Now, you're talking sick. *Sick* sick. Down and out, ugly, save-me-Lord, how-can-it-be-this-bad sick.

First, you have your fever. I didn't go to medical school, and maybe they explained this there, but how can a person feel cold when his body is running a high temperature? You're lying there under a heap of blankets, whimpering, and you're freezing.

About this time, you realize bad things are happening in tummyland. What it feels like, basically, is that two wolverines have burrowed inside of you and are wrestling for control of your stomach. It's hard to tell if it's their ripping and snarling at your stomach that hurts most, or their vicious claws digging at your other abdominal parts for better purchase.

Contemplating this, and the prospects of missing a pile of work at the office the next day, you fall asleep.

Is there anything worse than fever dreams?

It's like the guy running the projection booth in your brain says, "All right. Take off the Disney stuff. Put on some Fellini."

One time, in a fever, I dreamed I was in a writhing pile of sweaty NBA basketball players. Don't bother to analyze that dream for me, thanks.

The problem with a fever dream is that once you're in it, you can't get out. You dream the same dream for hours, possibly days. You dream you've woken up and gotten out of the dream, but, of course, that's just a dream. You can be in the same pile of basketball players for an eternity.

Then you wake up, and you are on fire. Your fever finally feels like a fever is supposed to feel. Get those blankets off. Throw a leg out to fresh air. Ah, relief.

Two minutes later, you're freezing again. Back under the blankets. Back to the fever dream.

Have we talked about total body aching yet? I didn't think so. At first, you think you simply might have been lying wrong in bed. But no, you've got the aches. You know it's bad when your hair aches. You crashed into the pillow several hours before, and now you wake up and you realize you've bent some of those follicles at unacceptable angles. You have the hair aches.

You are contemplating hair aches when you realize that face leeches have somehow invaded your sinus areas and have literally sucked all of the supporting liquids from around your eyes. Now, instead of eyes, you have two withered grapes barely clinging to your skull cavity. How about some light reading to pass the time?

Let's check in with the stomach again. Ah, great. The wolverines are gone. However, a family of ferrets has moved in for the scraps. Feel them scurry. Feel them slash and tear. Feel them gnaw.

It's time to get out of bed for a few moments. You try to stand, only to discover that the little people who run the gyroscopes in your inner ears, bored by your horizontal attitude for the past eight hours, have all taken vacations.

Watch the sick man walk. Watch him take itty-bitty steps. Watch him lean on the walls. Watch his emery-paper eyeballs squint at the glare of the bathroom night-tlight.

You make your appointed rounds, find enough walls to lean on to reach the bedroom again, and fall back in bed. Yes, this must be the right bed. The sheets are still hot.

You slither in, haul the covers up and join your fever dream in progress.

That's how it was when I was sick this week.

But I'm sure if you were sick, it was a lot worse.

Homecoming

It was Wednesday morning, and the food pack still wasn't unpacked from the previous week's canoe trip.

What is the deal, anyway? What is it about a vacation that makes you need a week's vacation *after* the vacation just to get your life back in order?

And while we're at it, I'd lobby for a week's vacation *before* the vacation just to get ready for the vacation.

For employment purposes, all three weeks would count as only one week of vacation. But all should be paid, of course. We wouldn't want to add the stress of a tight budget to an already hectic month, would we?

I flipped open the pack flap, and there it all was—the hot chocolate, the instant soups, the cheesecake mix, the powdered milk, the spice kit. It had been there since Sunday night, growing whatever culture it is that gives all post-trip food packs the same telltale aroma. Something between dried fruit and wet rope.

I started tossing salvageable commodities into a grocery bag.

Everything had been so peaceful out there. Our world had been a flat-rock campsite, a tent, fresh blueberries, stars, mist in the morning, and the walleye our eight-year-old caught. Even the transition to reality at a friend's cabin had been peaceful.

Sauna. Dock. A great horned owl calling from an island. Loons tuning up for the nightly symphony.

You would think there would be some way to ease this walk from the woods to the real world. You would think it would be possible to slide back into civilization instead of being dropped.

But, no.

Here's what happens Sunday night after vacation. The car is packed to the gills with a week's worth of sleeping bags, kids' blankets, cabin trash, a leaky sack of recycling matter, canoe paddles, and tangled fishing rods. And the food pack.

All of which needs to be put away, the sooner the better.

Simultaneously, you have two hungry kids, no milk, some questionable bread, no apple juice. God forbid you ever have a two-year-old to whom apple juice is the elixir of life and you are dropped back in a world without the stuff.

You also have a week's worth of mail (why is the VISA bill always on top?), a week's worth of stale newspapers, a kitten in serious need of human touch, and a lawn in which the clover is at the peak of its reproductive cycle.

Someone discovers the eight-year-old's day-camp form, which states that her name needs to be on *everything* she brings, including her underwear. Day camp starts Monday. At 8:15 A.M. Monday. She'll need a sack lunch, too.

All of the stuff from the car is now spread from back porch to kitchen to bedrooms. The cat is whining. The two-year-old still needs apple juice. The eight-year-old is distraught that Sarah, her friend, will likely miss opening day of day camp.

Someone has started waffles, the all-time bail-out meal. Someone else has bulldozed all the mail and paper off the table so it can be set for supper.

Then another major problem—there is only a dab of store-bought maple syrup for the waffles, which means the kids will have to possibly gag down some *real* maple syrup, which just doesn't taste right, especially if you're eight and especially if your friend might not be making it to day camp.

Oh, my.

That's how it was, Sunday night after vacation.

Now it was Wednesday, and there was an unidentifiable item coming out of the food pack. Hmmm. I held it up to the light. Bagels. Bagels in a plastic bag. Bagels wearing something blue-green and fuzzy, something that possibly medical science would find interesting.

I trashed it.

But, hey, we're under control. We have apple juice.

Baby–sitter blues

Well, we have had another family crisis.

Everything seemed to be floating along just fine. We were all healthy, the VISA bill was under control, and then—wham—our two top baby–sitters both graduated from high school.

We must have been crazy. How could any parents in their right minds become so dependent on two girls who would graduate from high school the same year?

My advice to starting-out parents—diversify. Stagger the ages of your baby–sitters.

It isn't that these graduates have retired from baby-sitting. It isn't that they've left town already. But, for some reason, they would rather work at summer jobs paying four or five dollars an hour than play hopscotch with a seven-year-old and change diapers on a sixteen-month-old for two dollars an hour.

What's the matter with kids these days? Now, here we are, the parents who waited to have children, celebrating our mid-life crisis, desperately needing a couple of hours alone together—and we're playing hopscotch and changing diapers.

One of our sitters—we'll call her Linda—we broke in when she was eleven. Linda was the first sitter our oldest child ever had. She started out sitting for just a couple of hours on an afternoon, then gradually worked up to the varsity— evening jobs.

We came upon a couple of other fine baby–sitters completely by accident. We had moved into a new house and had lived there for about six months. One afternoon, I went out with the chainsaw to trim some trees. My neighbor through the woods, thinking I might have been pruning his trees (it turned out I was), came over to inspect.

We had a nice chat, during which I learned he had daughters twelve and fourteen who were baby–sitters.

It was almost like discovering oil on your property. Baby– sitters. Two of them. Within a baseball toss of our back door.

Now one of them has graduated. She's spending the summer dipping ice cream and mixing malts. This fall, she'll be off to college.

If this baby–sitter business doesn't seem serious to you, it must be because you don't have kids. I was the same way for years.

Once you become a parent, good baby–sitters are almost as valuable as good fishing spots. You don't realize how much you value good sitters until another parent, reaching the depths of desperation, will ask you if you can recommend some sitters to her. You give her the names, of course. But it's like drawing someone a map to your favorite walleye reef. Deep in your heart, you know that someday you could call one of your favorite sitters only to find out she's committed to sitting for your friend.

Compounding the baby–sitter situation for us is that Phyllis and I tend to plan our dates at the last minute. We'll decide on a Friday night that we want to go out on Sunday night. Just a little date. Dinner and conversation. That's all we're asking for. We need a sitter from 5:30 to 9:00 P.M.

137

We start with the varsity sitters. One has grandparents in town. Can't do it. Another has to study that night.

OK. We go down the list. One after another, our sitters reject us. We take turns calling because it's too depressing getting rejected so many times.

It takes only about six of those calls before you figure that maybe you just aren't supposed to have a date that night. Ah, but we're flexible. It isn't working for Sunday? How does Saturday sound to you, honey? OK?

Hey, we don't have to live life on our own timetables. We'll work our social life around our baby–sitters' social lives. We start down the list again.

"Hi, Jenny? We know you're busy Sunday night, but how about Saturday? Yeah. Tomorrow night. You can? Oh, thank you. Thank you."

Now, two names have been scratched off the top of our list by graduation.

They're great kids. We went to their graduation parties a couple of weeks ago. Nice parties. Balloons. Food. The whole works.

We took the kids with us.

The cat's meow

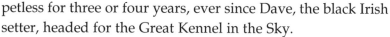

And so we got the cat. It's a '92 model, five weeks out of the factory. She has black and gray stripes, so, of course, the seven-year-old thought we should name her Freckles.

We did.

None of this came about without a lot of discussion. We had been petless for three or four years, ever since Dave, the black Irish setter, headed for the Great Kennel in the Sky.

As much as I'd like to have had a hunting dog during the petless era, I'll admit it was handy not owning an animal. No forced walks at 6:00 A.M. No hassles when it was time to go out of town. No critters drooling or spitting up or rolling on dead things.

But for more than a year, our seven-year-old daughter had been thinking she needed a pet. She had a two-year-old brother, but that didn't seem to be enough.

We knew she was desperate for a pet when she would fill balloons with water and ask us to tie them off. She would keep these water-balloon families for days at a time. They lived in a large bucket of water in the garage. Every now and then, we'd see the seven-year-old walking around petting something nestled in a towel in her arms. It would be a baby water balloon.

I suppose that having a cat now, we'll have more room in

our garage again.

Our daughter was more than reasonable on the pet issue. She was willing to compromise, knowing I would have preferred to get a hunting dog rather than a cat.

"We could get a hunting cat," she said.

But we didn't.

We got Freckles. Mostly, what Freckles has been hunting is some peace and quiet. We keep her there on the back porch with her water and her Cheerios—as the two-year-old calls her cat food—and her litter oil pan.

Yep. An oil pan.

The hardware store didn't have actual litter boxes.

"But a lot of people just use these oil drain pans," the man said.

So Freckles drains her oil in the big blue plastic saucer.

For solace, Freckles retreats behind the freezer, which has a warm motor—something like the mother she left behind, although I doubt her mother was that dusty. This worries the seven-year-old a great deal, who figures Freckles will catch on fire every time she goes behind the freezer. That's why the lawn chair and the life jackets are crammed into the nooks behind the freezer—to prevent Freckles from getting back there and turning herself into Crispy Critter.

Freckles, having sixteen or twenty of the sharpest claws on earth, merely climbs the life jackets or the lawn chair and retreats anyway. So far, we've smelled no burning fur.

The two-year-old conceives of Freckles as something like a baseball with legs.

He spends most of his time trying to put Freckles somewhere else, usually someplace about six inches higher than he can reach. On top of the dishwasher. On top of the dining room table. On top of the freezer.

He carries Freckles any way he happens to pick her up,

which is usually backwards. He uses the special cat-carrying technique known as the Death Grip.

The Death Grip is usually around the kitten's groin area, with the kitten's two back legs sticking out in front like a couple of furry antennas. Her head, meanwhile, dangles around the two-year-old's stomach. In this predicament, Freckles bugs her eyes wide open, and her eight or ten front claws paw the air for something to grip, which usually winds up being the two-year-old's tummy.

Oh, we're having a good time.

Saying no

I wish this week were unusual.

Monday night, it was the eight-year-old's piano recital.

Tuesday night, one of us had to work late.

Wednesday night, it was the eight-year-old's ceremony that would carry her from Brownie to Junior Girl Scouts.

Thursday, it was a dinner engagement with a friend.

Then, for good measure, we threw in one day of the car in the shop, closing on a home refinancing mortgage, and a day-long road trip for work.

And on the seventh day, we collapsed.

I don't recite this litany of too-much in order to single out our own family. I would guess it is much the same for many of us, maybe too many of us. Just substitute where necessary: Little League tryouts, a board meeting, a parent in a nursing home, a child under one, a wage-earner who travels all the time, a speech to a civic group, a church meeting, a niece's shower, hockey camp sign-ups, a grandson to baby–sit, a club program, a breakfast meeting, a project deadline.

It's clear to me. We're all too busy.

I was talking to an older woman the other day. She's eighty-five. I had gone to see her to talk about fishing, but we ended up talking about life. When you're eighty-five, you have a perspective that lets you see some things the rest of us don't see. And she could see we're all too busy.

"We had more time than you do now," she said. "It's such a different world now. Everyone is in a hurry."

This was a woman who raised five kids, including twins, and worked almost every day of her life. And she thinks we're too busy.

The problem is, how do you step off this not-so-merry-go-round? Even for an afternoon or an evening?

You say "no."

You don't say "no" because you have something else going on that evening. You say "no" because you don't want anything going on that evening.

I have gotten pretty good over the past few years at saying "no." I haven't gotten very good at saying "no" and not feeling somewhat bad about it.

I still think I should be able to do everything that comes my way. Lots of it I want to do—a morning canoe paddle, a three-day trip, a slide show for a friend's club. But I have learned a little bit. It is one thing to log these activities on the calendar. It is quite another to live through that week when it arrives.

I've found that when I say "no" and explain that I simply need the time for myself or my family, people understand. It seems to strike a chord with them. I think all of us would be better at saying "no" if we heard others say it to us more often for that reason—that we simply need to keep some quiet time in our lives.

And sometimes, we need to say it to ourselves.

The other day—one of those brimful days this week—I had raced home from a day on the road to pick up the kids at day care. It was a beautiful evening, the kind you get eight or nine of in Duluth every summer. The kids wanted to know if we could go to Canal Park after supper.

I said, "Sure."

We went home, walked the dog, fed the cat, scratched together a supper of leftovers, did the dishes, and helped the eight-year-old with her homework. Mom was gone, working.

I stood there, doing the dishes, looking out the window at the kids playing in the sandpile. I thought about driving down to Canal Park, spending forty-five minutes or so, driving home, giving baths, reading stories—another schedule. And I thought, "No."

We don't always have to go somewhere. We don't have to buy things. We don't have to be entertained, not even by a swirl of gulls overhead.

I walked outside in that beautiful evening light and I told the kids I had changed my mind, that we wouldn't be going to Canal Park.

The three-year-old came over and cried on my chest for a few minutes, but he recovered. It was a good night. Simple. At home in the yard with the sandpile and the dog and the bikes and the Big Wheels. Mom came home, and bath time went smoothly, and we had time to sit on the porch in the breeze before bedtime.

It was the best thing we could have done, not going somewhere.

And it was still hard to do.

Youth soccer and other parental rites of passage

Poked-out paranoia

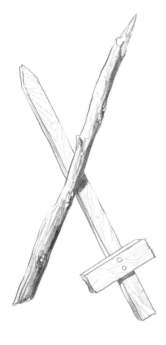

Welcome to today's class on Creative Parenting.

Today's subject is "Getting Your Eye Poked Out."

I don't know about you, but when I was growing up, it seemed like my parents were constantly harping at me not to do something because "you're going to poke somebody's eye out with that thing."

Near as I can tell, this warning was universal among 1950s parents.

We'd be playing pirate or cowboys or war with some harmless object like a sharpened stick or a barbecue fork or a broken-off fishing rod, and our parents would see us and sure enough, they would invoke the "poke somebody's eye out" warning.

I spent a good share of my formative years carrying an image in my mind of someone walking around with a hollow spot where his eye should have been. Yep. Someone got an eye poked out. Just like mom and dad said would happen.

As I saw it, getting an eye poked out was a real and present danger. It would happen so easily. You'd be pretending to duel a fellow pirate on the wooden frame of the sandbox and—pop—next thing you know, you'd be waving your brother's eyeball around on the end of your stick. He'd go running off to mom, and then you *were* going to be in trouble.

What happened, of course, is that after about three years and six hundred "poke somebody's eye out" warnings, you began to realize this was not likely to happen. Otherwise it would have happened already, right? You'd look around at your friends in class, and at your brothers' and sisters' friends when they came over. They all had two eyes.

They'd been playing pirate and war and cowboys and a million other combative games for several years and nobody had ever had his eye poked out.

But did our parents ever quit using the Eye-Poked-Out Scare? Of course not.

I'll bet I was fifteen or sixteen before my folks quit using that one on me. By then I'd taken up driving, and I suppose they had a lot more to worry about than a sharp-stick incident.

I am sure parents today still use the Eye-Poked-Out Scare. We can't help it. It's all subconscious or unconscious or whatever the correct psychiatric term is.

We see our kids playing with a piece of chrome they found in the garage and a tape is rewound in our brains and it just comes blurting out: "You kids quit playing with that thing before somebody gets his eye poked out!"

But, Creative Parents, observe how your children react to that command. These kids are being raised on laser warfare and Teenage Mutant Ninja Turtles. You think they're worried about something as ordinary as getting an eye poked out?

They just stare at you bewildered-like, with a look that says, "Give me a break, older dude. This isn't a piece of chrome. It's a Laser Destroyer Vacuum Imploder and I could wipe out your universe with one flick of its Action Module."

Eyes do not get poked out anymore. They get melted or gelled or mutated.

The way I see it, this makes two generations now for whom getting an eye poked out is, practically speaking, an empty threat. Our generation—the G.I. Joes. And the one we have begat—the Ninja Turtles.

From here on out, I respectfully suggest we never tell our kids that a hot fireplace poker might poke out their brother's eye.

No.

I would say that as Creative Parents we tell them something they can understand.

Like, "Don't you realize, honey, that if you don't put that poker down right now THE PULVERATOR WILL MATERIALIZE IN THIS ROOM INSTANTLY AND VAPORIZE YOU INTO A WORLD WITHOUT PIZZA?"

That should do it.

Gone fishin'

If you are looking for a good time, let a four-and-a-half-year-old and a five-year-old take you fishing.

I tried it the other night. The four-and-a-half-year-old was an Emily. The five-year-old was a Sarah.

"I'm gonna catch a salmon," Sarah said.

"I'm gonna catch a shark," Emily said.

"I'm gonna catch a salmon the size of a shark," Sarah said.

I've been in pickups with three adult men where the conversation has proceeded along roughly the same lines.

Emily had the Snoopy fishing rod, and Sarah took the ice-fishing rod with the old Zebco spincasting reel. They chattered all the way to the bait shop.

"Can we take the minnows home for pets?"

"I want to take home two minnows for my sisters."

"Yeah, Dad, can we take home some minnows?"

Fishing is a great way to get to know your kid. If we hadn't made this fishing trip, I probably wouldn't have heard our delightful, feminine daughter utter from the back seat: "At preschool, we say, 'Don't you dare touch my hair or you're dead meat.' "

At the bait shop, the debate was whether to buy minnows or leeches. If the five-year-old wants minnows, you can be sure her friend will want leeches. Bait shop owners love to see kids coming in pairs. We bought a dozen minnows and a dozen leeches.

Along the shore of Island Lake, we found a fishy looking stretch of pebbled beach. The Snoopy rod sent out a bobber, hook, and minnow. The ice-fishing rod went out with another minnow.

It was time for some serious fishing.

"Can I have some raisins?"

"Can I have some pretzels?"

"I'm thirsty. Can we have the apple juice now?"

We had raisins. We had pretzels. We had apple juice. We watched our bobbers.

Suddenly, the bobber on Emily's Snoopy rod began descending into the tannin-stained waters of Island Lake. This happened at a most inopportune time.

Emily had just grabbed a handful of raisins.

Emily was informed she had a bite. She was informed of this by a man who wanted nothing more than to grab that rod, yank that hook home, and pull in whatever was making the bobber disappear.

"OK, but I have to eat these raisins first," Emily said.

I explained to Emily that when you have a bite, you can't always finish what you're eating. You have to grab your Snoopy rod before the fishy pulls it into the lake.

"OK," she said.

So, with raisins dribbling out of her mouth and stuck to her cheek, she grabbed the rod and began reeling.

"I think I've got a fish," she said. "I think I've got a fish."

I think she did, too, except it got off at some point before the bobber reappeared, and the Snoopy reel retrieved an empty hook.

Oh, well. We impaled another minnow on the hook.

SARAH: "Oh, no! He's bleeding."

EMILY: "Yeah, he's bleeding."

DAD: "Yep. They usually bleed a little bit when the hook goes in."

SARAH: "Make him stop bleeding."

EMILY: "Yeah, make him stop bleeding."

DAD (CASTING): "He'll stop bleeding when he gets in that cool water."

And he might have. Who's to say?

We went for a long, biteless time. It was a warm, calm, perfect evening to be shore-fishing with a five-year-old and an almost-five-year-old.

"I hate leeches because—if you go in the water and you don't know there are leeches in there—they always stick to you."

"I wonder if I'm going to catch a fish."

"Will you show me the leeches?"

"Can we go home? I'm seasick."

"Hey! I just saw a flying fish."

We fished until the pretzels were gone, the apple juice had spilled twice, and most of the rocks on the beach had been excavated.

All in all, it was sort of wonderful.

Clothing Wars

The city looks peaceful on this weekday morning. The sun is rising over Lake Superior. Squirrels frisk about in the yards. Lawns are tidy.

But all is not quiet here. In the little bedrooms of the little houses in the orderly neighborhoods, wars are being waged.

Clothing Wars.

"I don't *want* to wear that!"

"I hate those pants!"

"That sweater is ugly!"

Yes, it's that delightful time of day. The kids are getting dressed for school.

What you have, on the one hand, is a grown-up person hulking in a child's doorway, baby on the arm, hair still amuss from a night's sleep. On the other hand, you have a small person kneeling in front of a dresser drawer, flinging its contents randomly to the bed, the light fixture, the toy box, and the floor.

The small person is looking for something to wear.

Add an air of urgency: There is the impending arrival of a

school bus or the neighbor kids, ready to whisk the small person schoolward.

"Well, what about that flowered blouse?" asks the grown-up.

"This one?" the child asks.

She lifts it out of the drawer, holding it as if it were crawling with ticks.

"I don't like this blouse. It doesn't feel right on me," she says.

"Well, I don't care what you wear," the grown-up says—lying—"but you'd better get dressed. Your friends will be here any minute, and if you're not ready, you'll have to walk to school alone."

Does this sound at all familiar? Or is there only one house of the thirty thousand or so in our tidy community where mornings are like this?

Why is it that you can spend a hundred dollars or more getting one kid outfitted for "Back to School" and by the time school actually rolls around, there's only one outfit the little munchkin wants to wear? That outfit is dirty, of course, because the small person was wearing it when (a) she was making mud-and-stick soup in the sandbox yesterday, (b) he needed something he could use for third base, or (c) she had it on for twenty seconds at breakfast before she spilled grape juice on it.

This leaves the small person with many other clothing choices, none of which is acceptable.

"Mommmmmm. I don't like the way turtlenecks feel on my neck."

"Mommmmm. That top doesn't go with those pants."

"Mommmmm. I can't wear a sweater. It's too hot in my room at school. I'll boil."

Sensing that the Zealous Supervision method of getting the child dressed isn't working, the grown-up leaves the kid's room and puts the child on his or her own. This is risky, but a desperate person takes desperate action.

Three minutes pass.

"I'm ready," the child announces, bouncing into the kitchen.

She is wearing blue slacks with pink and yellow hearts on them. She is wearing a turquoise and neon green and black sweatshirt with Mickey and Minnie Mouse on it. It's big at the neck, and her purple T-shirt shows from underneath.

The grown-up tries not to wince at this collision of color. But the small person did it herself, time is short, and there are more important things in the world, the grown-up is thinking.

"You look fine," the grown-up says. "Here's your lunch. Now get going."

So it goes, all across the city, as truces are declared in the Clothing Wars.

Lunch boxes are handed off. Backpacks are slung. Kisses are planted on small cheeks.

Another day is under way.

Or is it?

"Mom! Where are my shoes? I can't find my shoes!"

Don't worry. They'll find the shoes. The mud from last night's soccer game will be mostly dry in the soles. It will come out in neat little sole designs as the child walks across the living room to the front door.

The child, oblivious to both the tracks and the Clothing War itself, dances down the driveway full of whatever it is that makes kids skip, pet dogs, and compare lunch boxes on the way to school.

The grown-up slumps onto couch with baby.

And smells a diaper that wants to be changed.

Bracing
for the worst

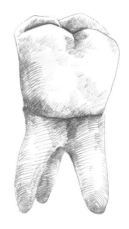

We should have known better.

We should have known that two lean-jawed humans who crossbreed would produce young with equally lean jaws. Maybe leaner.

All of this was brought home last week when our seven-year-old daughter visited the dentist. Like most normal seven-year-olds, every now and then she sheds a front tooth, which is replaced by one of those rough-edged permanent teeth barging through from above or below.

Trouble is, the tooth fairy is carrying off teeny little baby teeth, and they're being replaced by grown-up incisors. Word from the dentist last week was that she'll likely have to have some permanent teeth pulled to make room.

Not that we didn't have a warning about this.

When we first presented this little girl to the dentist for inspection at age two, the dentist had no sooner opened her mouth than out popped the pronouncement every parent loves to hear.

"Looks like you can count on orthodontia," the dentist said, still counting molars.

Like a lot of things dentists and doctors say, there's a less clinical term for the same thing. In this case, braces.

Oh, we know all about braces.

I wore braces.

Phyllis wore braces.

We dated with braces, and there were times during romantic moments when—well, we'd better leave it right there.

The point is, all of this could have been prevented if I'd only listened to Alphia Aberle.

Alphia was at that time a prosperous farmer in northeastern Kansas. I was a scrawny fourteen-year-old, and, as an act of charity, Alphia hired me to help him toss bales of alfalfa hay around his farm. I can remember taking a break somewhere in the rolling hay country, and Alphia asking me if I had a girlfriend.

I told him I was dating Phyllis Locher.

Now, in a small farm town, nearly everybody knows everything about everybody else—whether they drive Fords or Chevys, whether their soybeans and corn are free of weeds, and what shape their kids are.

Alphia knew what sort of stock Phyllis's folks produced, and he could see that it was all I could do with my pipe-cleaner arms to wrestle a sixty-pound bale of hay into submission.

I'll never forget what he said that hot Kansas afternoon.

"Phyllis Locher? Boy, you better get some meat in that cross somewhere," he said.

And we went back to baling hay.

That night, after I cleaned up, I got back to dating Phyllis and pretty much never quit.

It wasn't that I meant to disregard what Alphia had said; it's just that you really can't help who you're falling in love with. Staring into Phyllis's eyes in that '62 Ford, I never thought to drop my gaze and evaluate the cut of her jaw in an objective sort of way.

So, now we're all grown up, raising a fleet of skinny whelps of our own.

And bracing ourselves for orthodontia payments.

The saints
next door

Two mornings in a row, we deliberated over who would work and who would stay home.

Our third-grader was sick. She couldn't go to school. She couldn't go to day care with a fever. Each day, we had had to decide who could stay home and for how long.

It has become a familiar scene at our place this winter. We sit on the edge of the bed or circle around each other in the bathroom discussing the day's options.

"Well, I have to be at work this morning. I have to meet someone . . ."

"Could you be home by 1:00, do you think?"

"Yeah, that would work."

So, we tag-teamed through a couple of days, working half-days or bringing work home. I'm sure we weren't the only ones running this relay. Life must be this way in lots of homes these days where both parents work.

You wake up one morning and—wham—the flu has come to live with you. Suddenly, any semblance of routine the day had going for it is gone. Two minds do a mental tracery of the day as it was going to be. Appointments. Meetings. Deadlines.

The give and take begins. Who can miss what? Can we split up the day? Can either of us afford to miss the whole day of work? And what does that make the rest of the week look like?

It's a jolting way to start the day, but it's reality. Something has to give.

I don't mean to imply that taking care of a sick child is just another chore. When we brought kids into the world, we expected some of this duty. It comes with the territory. It's just a lot easier to schedule if the duty happens to fall on a Saturday or Sunday.

So, we went to bed that second night hoping recovery would occur during the hours of darkness.

No go.

Our daughter woke up sick for a third day. But at least her fever was gone, which meant she could go to day care.

She could lie on the couch at Marilyn's house, and we could both put in a full day of work.

At 6:45 A.M., the phone rang.

It was Marilyn. She had the flu. Sorry. No kids today.

We looked at each other. We danced the familiar dance of options. "Could you?" "Could *you?*" "Well, maybe a half-day."

It turned out both of us needed to be at work in the morning. There was nothing else to do. We would have to call Mel and Correen.

Mel and Correen live next door.

They're retired. We didn't know it when we bought our house, but Mel and Correen were the best part of the bargain. They are a couple of saints on loan for a lifetime here on earth.

Mel tills our garden. Correen cans raspberry jam for us. Mel takes out our trash when I'm out of town. Correen cans peaches for us. Correen and Mel painted the baby's room when he came early and ol' Dad was caught off guard.

You can try to get even with Mel and Correen. You can

snowblow their driveway once in a while, although it's hard to beat Mel at that game. You can mow part of their lawn once in a while, but their grown kids run a lawn service. It's hard to win that one, too.

About the best I can do is to drop some pheasants or fish off at their back door once in a while, but it seems a trifle compared to all they do for us.

Daylight was just breaking when we made the call.

Correen answered in a sleepy voice. She and Mel had planned to go paint at the church that morning, she said. But without hesitation, they changed their plans. Correen would go to the church and paint. Mel would come over for the morning and watch the kids.

What can you say about people like that?

You read the stuff in the paper these days and you think this old planet is falling apart at the seams.

And then someone drops a Mel and Correen into your life.

Saint Mel.

Saint Correen.

Right next door.

Angels for an hour

Maybe it is the sound of those tiny voices traveling the upper octaves as they bounce through "Jingle Bells."

Maybe it's all those grins with front teeth missing in ones and twos.

Maybe it's those rows of cherubic little faces, fresh-scrubbed and beaming, and those bright eyes searching the audience for the right set of parents.

Maybe that's what gets inside of me at the annual School Christmas Program.

No. I might as well be honest. All of that is part of it. But I went to these programs before *my* kid was one of those with the gap-toothed grins and the timid voices and the searching eyes. It was always good. But it was never like this.

I watched nieces and nephews and never got that feeling in my throat or the wetness in my eyes. Here they come now, into the gymnasium, where the construction-paper Christmas trees have been taped to the wall, the construction-paper chains have been draped behind the risers and the construction-paper poinsettias twist in the breeze below the light fixtures.

Here they come, wearing self-conscious grins and walking single-file through the hearts of those who have come to sit on the folding chairs and admire them.

Here they come, with crisp Christmas dresses and handsome little-man sweaters and hands strictly to themselves. They are pure and innocent and clean.

Never mind that the girls will screech at the top of their lungs at recess if they get boy germs on their hands, or that the boys know so well how to inspire the rage of a younger sister at home, or that either gender would rather eat asparagus than take a bath. For this hour in December, with piano accompaniment, they are all angels.

There, on the risers, under the basketball goal, they open their little mouths in unison and what comes out is a kind of music heard nowhere else. It's soft and sweet and at least two octaves higher than the composer had in mind. If you are a parent of one of the small people making this sound, it touches something inside of you that does not get touched often.

There is something in the sound of children's voices that, when I close my eyes, makes me believe I could be in Africa or the Philippines or Iraq. Like music, kids bear a kind of universal message about hope and joy and life.

Then I open my eyes and see the construction-paper chain falling down behind a tall kid on the back row of the risers. Happens every time. Something falls. Somebody starts the second verse a little early. The kindergartners have no apparent notion that the piano is playing the same song they are singing.

I like that. I like imperfection in a program. I like at least the possibility of imperfection.

I like first-graders waving to their parents in mid-"Jingle Bells." I think I might attend more symphonies if I thought there was a chance the bass player would give a big ol' wave to his wife or kids during a slow spot in Beethoven's Fifth.

The little people are filing out now, taking last glimpses over their shoulders at parents with rolling camcorders. Now the fourth- and fifth- and sixth-graders are filing in, and I am stunned at how grown-up they appear.

Because, of course, they are.

They sing out. They spend more time in the customary octaves. They are not so coy about finding their parents in the audience.

These are the big kids. The ones who little kids regard with awe. The ones who monitor the halls. The ones who ensure safe street crossings.

As a group, the big kids don't stir me quite the way the young ones do.

But, I remind myself, maybe it is because I am looking at all of them, not one of them.

Kick it!

Well, we had the big post-soccer-season pizza bash this week, which marked the end of another youth soccer season.

It was a good season, I think, but then with soccer you can't really tell.

You can't tell because you grew up playing hockey or basketball or baseball, and you don't have the slightest idea of what your kid is supposed to do on a soccer field.

Which is the ideal kind of kids' sport, when you think about it, because you don't have a bunch of know-it-all parents standing on the sidelines yelling, "Hey ump, that was a strike!" Or, "You've got to sag on the big man in that zone."

No. All we soccer parents know how to yell is, "Kick it! Kick it!"

Farther into the season, we get more sophisticated, of course. We yell, "Kick it, John!" or "Kick it, Ashley!"

Every now and then an adolescent male roughly three soccer balls taller than anyone else on the field blows his whistle. That would be the referee. In a voice audible only to the kids on the field, the referee says something.

There is some general milling around, and then someone throws the ball into play or kicks it from someplace significant only to the referee.

166

None of us on the sidelines knows what the call is for, so we go on talking about bears in our garbage and gas mileage of minivans and crappie fishing trips, occasionally yelling, "Kick it, Ben!"

There is always one parent who is actively involved in the game. That person is the one who got guilted into being the Flag Person. This person stands right up on the out-of-bounds line and raises a little flag if the ball rolls out of bounds. The referee, who can plainly see the ball has rolled out of bounds, rarely looks at the Flag Person, but all of the other parents are quick to critique the Flag Person's style.

"Nice flag work, Sue."

Or, "Let's be a little quicker, Frank."

You feel mostly like a dolt doing it anyway and even more doltish because the referee pays you so little attention.

The only way you can get out of being Flag Person is to ask your spouse to do it while you go watch your two-year-old play on the playground equipment, which is so far from the field that your eight-year-old looks about the size of a Nintendo character.

I was Flag Person once this year, and I was taking a lot of pride in my work.

I had good wrist action. My flag came up fast and flew high. When the ball rolled out on my side of the field, there was no doubt it was out of bounds—my flag said so.

Once, a ball was kicked out of bounds in a flurry of eight-year-old feet and shin pads, right in front of me. Up went my flag. The referee, in an unprecedented move in my three years of soccer observation, came over and asked me, "Was that off of Green or White?"

Huh?

They never told me we were supposed to see who touched it last. I told the ref I didn't know.

"OK, then we'll have a jump ball," he said.

Or maybe it was a drop ball. Or a face-off. Or a curve ball. Heck, I don't know.

Bright moments do occur in the life of a soccer parent, and one of the most enjoyable is listening to what the kids say as they come off the field. One girl came running off at the end of her shift, looked up at me and said, "My dad broke his elbow today."

Which he had.

During the season's final game, one girl came running off and said, "Do we have to win to get free pizza at the pizza party?"

Once, when my daughter and I were discussing a game in the car on the way home, she blurted out, "You know when we go through that line and shake hands with the other team after the game? Some of those boys on the other team really slap your hand hard."

Which, having been a boy once myself, I'm sure is true.

But that's all over now. We had the big pizza party, which, in effect, turns a normal restaurant into a gymnasium that smells like pepperoni. The kids were arm wrestling and yelling and grabbing and having a good time. I'm sure our own little soccer player was having fun. I went over to ask her if she was getting plenty of pizza to eat.

"Yeah, Dad," she said. "But Matt's burping in our faces."

And she giggled.

Like I say, it was a good season all the way around.

Peanut butter cups

A Sunday night, and I'm on the trail of Reese's Peanut Butter Cups. Thirty of them, to be exact.

No, it is not an addiction. It's simply that our eight-year-old needs them for treats in school Monday morning, to celebrate her birthday with her class, and we have been gone all weekend.

"Peanut butter cups, Dad. And if you can't get those, get Tootsie Roll Pops," the eight-year-old said.

Those were my orders. And she hustled off to bed, trusting that I would come through for her while she slept.

The car's headlights probe the fog like a pair of pale laser beams. The first grocery store is closed. I forge ahead to another. Peanut butter cups. Gotta have 'em.

I drive along in the cold June fog, pondering my place in life.

I am aware that much of what I do now is like this Reese's quest. It's done for the little people in my life. I put my own needs and wants on hold to make sure those of my kids are met.

I'm not complaining, understand, and I have plenty of help from my wife.

Still, ten or twelve years ago, I never would have envisioned driving the streets at 9:30 P.M. on a Sunday looking for the mother lode of peanut butter cups.

All of this came on gradually, of course. I remember when our first child was born. I think I was in a large state of denial about children. I vowed that having kids wouldn't change my life. I had heard so much from other parents about how children had done that to their lives.

Nope. Not us, I thought. We'll be different.

So, we took our first child camping—to the canoe country—when she was six weeks old. We fished with her slung on our chests. We skied with her slung on our backs.

(I did try playing volleyball once while wearing my month-old daughter on my chest, but after a couple of dives for wayward balls, my wife saw me and pulled me out of the game.)

I guess I was trying to make a point. People—older and wiser—would ask if having a kid had changed our lives.

No, I'd tell them. It really hasn't.

Then, five years later, we had a second child. Oh, I thought. *This* is what they were talking about.

There was no more denying it. My life had changed. More and more often, I would miss going for a run because I felt it was important to have dinner with the family. More and more often, I would postpone preparing for a road trip until the last minute because I wanted to spend that final afternoon with my wife and kids. Finally, even the length of the trips began to shrink because I simply didn't want to be gone from my family for as long as I had been before.

I keep thinking, based on those decisions, that I've passed through the denial stage and have arrived at the acceptance stage.

I understand now when there are diapers that need to be changed when I'm halfway through a bowl of Shredded Wheat.

I have accepted that in order to put a pair of shoes on a three-year-old I am going to be involved in a high-speed chase.

I know that if the decision is between the soccer game or my bike ride, it will be the soccer game.

The only thing that makes me question my progress is that I keep thinking this is all a temporary thing. I keep thinking life will return to what I once thought was "normal."

But I might as well face it. This is forever.

I approach the second grocery store. The red letters of its sign come glowing through the fog. The store is open. It is well-stocked with Reese's Peanut Butter Cups. I make my buy.

It is a simple thing, I know. But driving home, I cannot help feeling a disproportionate sense of satisfaction that I have come through for my kid.

I get my kicks in unexpected places these days.

Life is sweet

Matters of the heart **174**

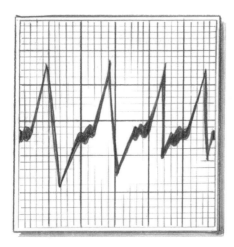

Matters of the heart

I think it was the way the gull looked at me. That and the images of my wife and kids that kept appearing in my mind.

I was sitting on a sand dune on Minnesota Point, wondering if maybe, possibly, crazily, something was going haywire in my heart.

A mile and a half into a noon-hour run, the feeling had begun to grow in my chest. Not pain. Not the proverbial elephant sitting on one's chest. But something unusual, a tightness I hadn't felt before.

So I walked for a bit, then sat down on the dune. I'd been there four or five minutes when the gull flew over. He wasn't ten feet above me and I remember his head rotating back and forth to look me over, as if maybe I was something to eat. I was feeling vulnerable and confused and scared already.

That did it. I didn't want to *become* gull food. I walked to the nearest house to ask a couple if they'd call an ambulance. The man squinted at me.

"Are you serious?" he asked.

Yes, I told him.

"OK, OK," he said. "We get a lot of crazies down here."

Three weeks have passed since that noon run. New words have come into my vocabulary, words I never wanted to learn. Angiogram. Circumflex artery. Echocardiogram.

And the two biggies: Heart attack.

Heart attack. Me.

Crazy.

It shouldn't have happened to me, the doctors say. I have no risk factors, they say. After another month, I should be doing everything I used to do, they say.

I believe them. I want to believe them. I do my walks and my bicycling and my slow runs and wait until I can get on the treadmill in mid-June to see what kind of heart I have left.

And, like every woman who has felt a lump in her breast and every man who has felt the tightening in his chest, I don't look at life the same way anymore.

I remember standing at the window of room 656 at St. Mary's Medical Center, watching people cross the street, watching cars come and go at the stoplight, watching the boaters troll Lake Superior for trout and salmon.

They are lucky, I recall thinking. Lucky to be outside. Lucky to be crossing a street. Lucky to be driving and fishing.

Lucky to not be umbilicaled to a machine down the hall tracing their heartbeats in green blips. Lucky to not be fussed over twenty-four hours a day. Lucky to not have had a cardiologist sit at their bedside and say, "There are three bad things that could happen during this test. One is a stroke. One is a heart attack. The third is you could die."

I didn't come close to dying. Not during the test. Not even that day sitting on the sand dune. My heart attack was mild, they tell me. Had I not turned myself in to medical authorities, I might well have recovered on my own and not been sure I had suffered the attack.

But I had brushed close enough with death to lie awake in

a hospital bed wondering what might have been—and what might be.

The vulnerability I felt in room 656 hangs on. It has eased somewhat, but it is still there. You lie in bed, feeling your heart thumping against the mattress, and you find yourself thinking, "Yeah. That's the way. Keep it up, ol' buddy."

You never thought of that before.

Your daughter crawls up on your lap and snuggles against you and you smell her hair. As much as you've enjoyed the hundreds of times that's happened before, it is far more precious now. You nuzzle her. And you wonder.

Your baby boy is crying, and you lift him from his crib. The crying becomes a whimper and the whimper becomes a smile of gums. You are aware of how much that little critter is counting on you. And you wonder.

That is what I think about these days.

In spite of the wondering, in spite of the lingering vulnerability, every day is a good day. A big day at work? I can handle it. A sick child? I'm ready. Traffic backed up at 5:00 P.M.? Small potatoes.

Life is sweet.

Get out there. Dance with your kid. Snuggle with your sweetie. Watch the flight of a gull.

Be thankful.

Pfeifer-Hamilton, a small publishing house located in Duluth, Minnesota, creates quality gift books that celebrate the beauty, heritage, and people of our country and the skills of the Northland's finest authors and artists.